KLONDIKE
Cattle Drive

KLONDIKE
Cattle Drive

The Journal of Norman Lee

Prepared for publication by Gordon Elliott,
with a foreword by Eileen Laurie

VICTORIA • VANCOUVER • CALGARY

TouchWood Editions
#108 – 17665 66A Avenue
Surrey, BC V3S 2A7
www.touchwoodeditions.com

Library and Archives Canada Cataloguing in Publication
Lee, Norman, 1862-1939
   Klondike cattle drive: the journal of Norman Lee / prepared for
publication by Gordon Elliott; with a foreword by Eileen Laurie

ISBN 1-894898-14-1

   1. Lee, Norman, 1862-1939—Diaries. 2. British Columbia—Description
and travel. 3. Yukon Territory—Description and travel. 4. Cattle drives—
British Columbia. 5. Cattle drives—Yukon Territory. I. Title.

FC3817.2.L33 2005   917.11   C2005-904132-3

Book design by Frances Hunter
Cover design by Erin Woodward
All photos courtesy of Anne and Vicky Lee

Printed in Canada

TouchWood Editions acknowledges the financial support for its publishing
program from the Government of Canada through the Book Publishing Industry
Development Program (BPIDP), Canada Council for the Arts, and the British
Columbia Arts Council.

The Canada Council | Le Conseil des Arts
   for the Arts | du Canada

BRITISH COLUMBIA
ARTS COUNCIL
We acknowledge the support of the Province of British Columbia
through the British Columbia Arts Council

Printed on 100% post-consumer recycled paper.

Contents

Notes on the 2005 Edition

The design for this edition is based on the original 1960 design by Robert R. Reid for Mitchell Press. Reid, who had his own press at the time and was producing finely printed limited editions on British Columbia history, approached Howard Mitchell about co-publishing the book after Reid's wife heard Eileen Laurie reading parts of Norman Lee's journal on her CBC morning program. Reid was involved in the composition of the metal type for the 1960 edition, using the typeface El Dorado. The digital form (now spelled Eldorado) is used in this edition.

As in the previous editions, Norman Lee's journal has been left unaltered. This new edition features photographs recently provided by the Lee family, and an update by Gordon R. Elliott to his original introduction of 1960. At the end of that introduction, Gordon had briefed readers on the whereabouts of Norman Lee's descendents. Since then, of course, many changes have occurred.

Norman Lee's son Daniel died in 1979, and Dan's wife Margaret in 1971. Norman's brother E. P. ("Young Lee") passed away in 1960. In 1989 the Lee ranch was divided among Norman's grandchildren, Norman ("Brud") Lee, Robin Lee and Wendy Lee Fletcher. Wendy and her husband Brian sold their share in 1999 and now live at 150 Mile House. Brud, his wife Anne, and Robin Lee and his wife Cindy continue to live on their grandfather's ranch. Anne and Brud are the proud keepers of Norman Lee's original journal, and all other memorabilia that once belonged to this famous pioneer of the Chilcotin.

Foreword

In that vast inland portion of British Columbia known as "The Cariboo," the name of Lee is almost legendary. But it meant nothing to me when I stepped off the train in Quesnel in June of 1948. My mission was to open an art show.

During my three-day visit, the name of Norman Lee kept recurring. His epic attempt to drive 200 head of cattle to the Klondike goldfields in 1898 was a favorite saga of the old-timers, and they told me that he had recorded his perilous adventure in a diary. Norman had died nine years before, but presumably his journal was still in the possession of his family.

I didn't pursue the story at the time, as the Lees lived many miles away, at the little cross-roads settlement of Hanceville, in what is known as "Chilcotin Country." Had anyone told me then that within the next ten years I would become a close friend of the Lee family, and be intimately involved in the publication of Norman's diary, I should certainly have wondered how such a thing could come about. But it did.

Having long been interested in the many untold tales of British Columbia pioneers and hoping to publicize some of them, I began an experiment in 1953, in my capacity as morning commentator for the Canadian Broadcasting Corporation. My program was broadcast over a province-wide network five days a week, Monday through Friday. One morning I announced that henceforth Wednesday's broadcast would be "listeners' day." I asked for authentic stories and eye-witness reports of experiences that would help us to know each other.

The response was immediate. The Wednesday morning show became a feature to which we all looked forward. A listener in northern B.C. dubbed it "Party Line," because, she said, "we all listen in." In June of 1954, thanks to *Party Line*, I received a story from a Mrs. Agnes Lee of Hanceville, describing her introduction to the ranchlands of British Columbia in the dead of winter, 1903. She was Norman Lee's widow.

A short time later, Mrs. Lee came to Vancouver for a specialist's advice on her failing eyesight. I interviewed her on the air—and afterwards, over several cups of tea, asked her many questions about her late husband's diary.

"You must come and visit us," she said, "then you can read it."

The following summer, my husband and I accepted her invitation and drove through the fabulous grasslands of the Chilcotin to the old log house to which Norman Lee had brought his bride more than half a century before. Since Norman Lee's death in 1939, his widow (affectionately known as "Gan-Gan" throughout the region) and their son Dan had carried on, in true pioneering spirit building up one of the Cariboo's largest herds of purebred Herefords. The Lees were also doing a thriving business with tourists and Indians in the trading centre across the road from the house.

The store was another log structure, its hand-hewn door flanked on both sides by aged but still colourful totem poles.

Step inside that door, and you are in another world. Reminiscent of those early days are the blocks of salt ... coils of rope ... stacks of wide-brimmed cowboy hats ... bolts of bright cotton prints ... a table

The original store at Lee's Corner

Gan-Gan and Daniel Lee

piled high with buckskin moccasins and gloves ... cooking utensils
... lanterns and various kinds of harness hanging from the rafters ...
gay embroidered and fringed jackets made by the Chilcotin Natives.
Even the gas pump at the foot of the well-worn steps outside is from
another generation. In the loft are bales of furs.

The Lee ranch house (the first unit of which is "the chicken
coop" in Norman's journal) was added to several times during his
lifetime. Today it presents a mellowed picture of peaceful living,
surrounded by a truly lovely garden that is the special delight of

Norman's daughter-in-law, Margaret. Stuck between the palings of the fence are several bleached cattle bones, facetiously inscribed by Norman as "dinosaur relics, dug up nearby." Norman Lee's sense of humour stayed with him to the end of his days.

He had arrived in San Francisco and had eventually worked his way north to Yale, B.C., which was the end of navigation on the Fraser River and the "jumping-off place" for the Cariboo. There Norman met hundreds of men virtually begging their way back to civilization. It wasn't easy to find a job, but for a while he was foreman of a crew of Chinese workmen who were shovelling rocks off the CPR right-of-way, as the head of steel was pushed through the Fraser Canyon to the Pacific coast.

Being young and full of ambition, Norman Lee hoped for something better than this—perhaps a ranch of his own. So he moved to Kamloops, where he worked a short time for the Hudson's Bay Company and met another young adventurer, named Bayliff. Shortly afterwards, the two of them set off over the rough Cariboo Trail with its dust and ruts, bogholes, slow-moving ox-teams and the stagecoaches of the famous Barnard's Express.

Norman and his friend made many side trips off the main trail in search of the right kind of ranch. They went into the Chilcotin as far as Redstone, where Bayliff decided to settle. But Norman preferred the area some forty miles east—a place called Hanceville. Here he purchased his "chicken coop" cabin, and a store from a man named Ole Norberg.

For years, Norman kept digging up ten- and twenty-dollar gold pieces that Norberg had buried in the flour bin, the tea chest, the rice barrel and other odd places. Norman soon established a brisk trade among the trappers, settlers and Natives of the Chilcotin area.

During my first visit to the Lee ranch, I read Norman Lee's journal and marvelled at his vivid and humorous accounts of his own "Trail of '98," and chuckled over his cartoons and sketches. Gan-Gan gave me permission to read excerpts on *Party Line* and long before the readings were concluded, requests began coming in for copies of the scripts. Then Gan-Gan suggested that perhaps we might have it published. She appointed me as her agent.

In December 1958, while negotiations for publication were still in the planning stage, Gan-Gan passed away in her 87th year. As a memorial to this grand old lady who had become my friend, I reread on the air the story she had written for *Party Line*, and again many requests were received for script copies. So I think it is only fitting that her own story should be included.

"We first arrived in Canada on January 19th, 1903, after a rough passage across the Atlantic. Not being a good sailor, I was glad to set foot on good, solid earth again. Our voyage had been made more pleasant by the appearance of Madame Albani and her concert party, though several of them, like myself, suffered from seasickness and were not at all anxious to keep their concert engagement the night we landed in Halifax.

"Norman and I went down to see Niagara Falls, then began our long journey westward by train. There were triple windows in the sleeping cars, yet the snow drifted through them all. We visited briefly at Boissevain with my brother and family, then left for Ashcroft, B.C. Norman went on ahead of me to try and get to his home and bring down a team and sleigh to meet me at Ashcroft. But as it happened, his brother Penrose was already there awaiting our arrival, so Norman wired me and I left next day. My train was snowed in for two days, somewhere near Banff, so it was February 10th when I arrived at Ashcroft. It was fifty below zero. Next morning we started on our long sleigh ride of two hundred miles to Hanceville.

"At various points along the way, Norman would stop and build a fire from small trees he cut by the roadside, to thaw me out. This seemed a terrible thing to me, as one doesn't just casually burn trees that don't belong to you in England.

"The first house we stopped at, the lady advised me to take off my shoes and put my feet right up against the stove. Never having seen this type of stove before, I took her at her word—and left part of my stockings on her lovely polished range. At our next stop the hired girl had just left to be married. The poor lady of the house (which was crowded with five children) had to attend to an enormous pile of dishes after supper. I told her to put the children to bed and I'd do the dishes. They were piled sky-high, and I'd never washed dishes before in my life.

"In the meantime, Norman always had to phone ahead for the stabling of the horses. It didn't seem to matter about people. They could sleep on the floor if necessary. But horses were important.

"Next day our hosts were bachelors. As Norman and I were newlyweds, they insisted we move into their nice 'annex.' There hadn't been a fire in it all winter, so when the stove was lighted, the frost came out and literally poured down the walls. You could have wrung the water out of the sheets.

"Finally we came to the Fraser River. It was frozen, so we crossed on the ice. When we came to the ferryman's house, I noticed that his wife was English and asked what part she came from. She said, 'Oh, you wouldn't know. It's a little place called Chorley, in Somerset.' Well, my cousin happened to be the rector of Chorley at that time, so the ferryman's wife and I became friends at once.

"Early next morning, Norman and I went on our icy way. And after seven days of sleigh-riding from Ashcroft we finally arrived at Hanceville. There was a house built of logs in the midst of a wilderness, with a trading post just across the road. This was my home in the New World.

"Having come straight from an English drawing room, I was soon very homesick. Especially when Norman talked pidgin English to the Chinese cook and various dialects with the Indians. But I never let him know I was unhappy in the home he had provided for me. Riding was one of my greatest joys in this strange new world, and I often rode out to the Old Indian cemetery nearby. There I'd sit on the rail fence and cry my heart out. Had there been cars or planes at that time, I probably wouldn't be writing this! But now I wouldn't change my life for anything in the world.

"The Indians in the Chilcotin country became wonderful friends, and I came to know them really well during the next fifty years. One day a very old Indian came to our store and I went and sat beside him. He told me he was a hundred and five years old. After a bit of gossip he said, 'Your canned goods are all frozen.' I replied, 'None of them are. We keep two stoves going all night in the store.' He said, 'Oh, yes, they're froze. Suppose you sell 'em. They kill a man.' I turned away, but he called me back. 'Suppose you sell 'em half price. Okay?' We did not do business!

"Later there was a Native woman who frequently came to our store to purchase supplies and exchange local gossip. She always sat against a counter that held two large spools of rope, the ends of which stuck out through a hole in the front. This aged woman was always wrapped in a blanket, and we noticed that she frequently stood up to rearrange her blanket around her. When it came time to close the store that night, she seemed much fatter than when she came in, and we discovered she was carrying some forty pounds of rope wrapped around her generous middle.

"Well, gradually I settled into my new life and learned how to deal with its many problems. Norman Lee was a wonderful husband whose knowledge of the country and never-failing sense of humour soon changed me from a hothouse flower into a sturdy pioneer wife, more than fifty years ago."

Through my friendship with the Lee family I came to know Penrose, Norman's only surviving brother, who has been a rancher in the Chilcotin country for more than fifty years. By accident, Penrose found part of a letter written twelve years before by Bill Copeland, the only man on Norman's expedition who stayed with him to the end. When last heard of, he was living in Kelowna, B.C. During the summer of 1958 I went there to find him and spent an entrancing evening listening to his stories of Norman and their historic trek. Bill had just passed his 89th birthday, but seemed more like a man in his sixties. Thin and wiry, with sparkling eyes and vivid memories, he talked for more than two hours about his "boss" and their adventures together.

"I always liked Norman," he said. "If Norman thought any of the men were better acquainted with a particular job, he'd turn it over to them. When we were travelling together, he always had me pick the camping place. He found I was good in the woods and not afraid to travel alone. No, I never carried a gun. All the wild animals I met were as much afraid of me as I was of them, or more."

I wish I could have met Norman Lee.

Eileen Laurie
Vancouver, British Columbia, 1960

Norman Lee, his wife Agnes (Gan-Gan) and son Daniel

Update to the Original Introduction

In my introduction to the earlier editions of *Klondike Cattle Drive: The Journal of Norman Lee*, I mentioned Mr. Lee's taking kids in his car from Williams Lake for a holiday on his ranch in the Chilcotin. I was several times one of those kids who gasped as Mr. Lee drove too fast and too close to the huge boulders scattered across Becher's Prairie. I was also one of those kids who happily read the books Mr. Lee pressed us to read and one of those kids to whom he talked so easily and grammatically that none of us have ever forgotten him. By 1959 he had become part of our own pasts. I recall once promising him that I would someday write something about the cattle industry in British Columbia, and yet I've never done so. I did not know so early in my life how difficult writing can be.

Besides, as we grow older we adjust our memories: our lives change and we move on. Our older views become twisted. For instance, one day in 1946 I rode a horse from Riske Creek in the Chilcotin to Williams Lake and noticed, when on Becher's Prairie, while that wild unbroken mare was trying to brush me off or scrape me from her back, that none of those boulders were as large as I had remembered them from the mid-'30s. Had something happened to them? Or, over those few years, had I seen boulders even bigger?

Now, 45 years after that first edition of his journal, apart from my description of Norman Lee as a small, athletic man with a kind heart and a sense of humour, I believe that a good introduction should have pointed out something in his journal that reflects some of his views and his attitudes. Being a modest man, he never really "underlined" many of them and as a result different readers like him for different reasons.

I, for one, recognize and admire Norman Lee's racial tolerance and attitude toward the Indians he employed at a time when there was less tolerance than there is today. When the cook Tabby became ill, Mr. Lee appointed one of the Indians as cook, one of the most important people in the crew; and he almost immediately tells of Indians who, like White men, had fenced in some kind of ranch. This extremely well-educated Englishman had his own store in Hanceville and did well by using an Indian sense of trading. But he also sold rum.

One comes to realize that his sense of humour is decidedly wry. Think of those "pilgrims" being on the "the main road to the golden north ... They were evidently prepared for war, as hardly a man passed but was hung all over with six shooters and bowie knives." Pilgrims prepared for war? Armed pilgrims? But he also has thoughts on churchmen. And the response when he talks of "intelligent" governments building roads and misplaced bridges: what else is new? But the dance on a Stoney Creek "rancherie" makes fun of Whites and Indians alike.

The wit carries on to the end, but the reader is also introduced to the subject of money. No one should think that money-grubbing is new to society today. Prices were high whenever money mattered, and that was anytime, anywhere. Yes, but we must remember that he himself has told us that he was there because of money. Was he ahead of his time?

But like fewer of us today, he took life in his stride. Willing to start all over again, with his dog Robert—nicknamed Bobber—Norman Lee hurried home to the Chilcotin from his costly adventure ... "and the band played Annie Rooney." He was a thinker ahead of his times and we should read him carefully. I'm glad I met him when I did.

Gordon R. Elliott
Vancouver, British Columbia, 2005

Introduction

The legend of Norman Lee is derived from his journal, from his letters, and from the men who accompanied him when he attempted to herd his cattle from the Chilcotin northward to the Klondike, where, in 1898, people from all the world were panning for gold in the rivers of the fabulous Yukon district. He braved the distances and the hazards, and he gambled his cattle and his life. He drove a herd of cattle overland, for a thousand miles as the crow flies. For the first time in twelve years, he had seen an opportunity to safeguard his investment and a possibility of making enough money to visit his family in England. This journal, his own, tells of the adventure.

In 1897 news of increased gold discoveries in the Klondike was welcomed generally by an economically stagnant world, but welcomed particularly by those cattle ranchers struggling for a living on the Chilcotin plateau of British Columbia. During the 1860s ranches had developed in the lower Chilcotin to supply the Cariboo mining areas with cattle, but the gold rush was short-lived and as the disappointed Argonauts had left Barkerville—the chief town—so had the market for beef. However, a decade and more later, Canadian Pacific Railway construction crews required meat and bought first close at hand and later from Dog Creek, Empire Valley and Alkali Lake. This attracted to the more northerly and westerly areas of the

Chilcotin occasional settlers like Norman Lee, who dreamed of becoming cattle barons. But with the completion of the railroad, the local market again disappeared. For men in the upper Chilcotin, the coast market was still too small and far away, although one could drive to Ashcroft and ship south on the newly constructed line.

In 1897 they saw a chance to cut losses (their select three-year-olds brought only $18 to $20); they began to talk of drives to the Klondike, and to Dawson City particularly, where hordes of miners were congregating—miners who required meat and who had the money to pay for it. Unfortunately, the gold-bearing region was beyond some of the world's roughest country.

Safety and common sense seemed to designate overland drives, and this belief was strengthened by rumours that animals shipped from Seattle, Vancouver, Victoria or Nanaimo and then unloaded at Skagway could never be moved over the Chilkoot and other passes. The overland route from the Chilcotin to this latest Eldorado would probably go up Alexis Creek and along the Nazko River to meet the Telegraph Trail. This trail was cut by the Collins Overland Telegraph Company, which was to have been part of a telegraph line from New York to London by way of San Francisco, Siberia and Moscow. The slashing had been completed only to Telegraph Creek, and the line had been strung only to Quesnel when the project was abandoned because a cable was laid successfully across the Atlantic. Built between 1865 and 1867, even the Telegraph Trail would be of questionable character by 1898, and beyond Telegraph Creek, which was only halfway, travel would become even more difficult.

Nevertheless, like some others, Norman Lee could not "see much chance to lose anything" and, as he wrote to his sister, Grace Alder Lee, "one might make a good deal." He himself had the required nerve; he had fifteen years' experience in the country; he knew the people and he knew their ways. Trusted, he trusted others. He also had something to which to return: he had his ranch, he had his store. That hard winter of 1897–98, he made his plans and in May, with hired men and his strongest stock, he was ready to begin the long drive, 1,500 miles and more, northward to Dawson City rather than 185 miles southward to Ashcroft and railhead.

Athletic, 5 feet 8 inches, 185 pounds, built for such a trip, he had been born in the village of Morland, Westmorland, on October 18, 1862, the son of Matthew Henry Lee, a graduate of Oxford, vicar of the parish and canon of the diocese. His mother was Scottish. Like his two younger brothers, Norman Lee was educated for Marlborough at Hartfordhouse, where the curriculum was predominantly classical. From this school run by his uncle, the Rev. Thomas William Lee, he entered Haileybury and later was apprenticed to an architect. His brother, Robert Warden Lee, who died in 1958, became a Fellow of All Souls, Oxford, and was once Dean of Law at McGill University. Edward Penrose Lee came to the plateau two years after his brother Norman. Some years later a sister, Helen Warden Lee, also came to Chilcotin; the other sister, Grace Alder Lee, apparently remained in England.

Inactivity in the architect's office bored Norman. An adventurous youth, he had been reading the books then circulating about the exciting Cariboo gold rush, and he knew that gold was supposedly abundant in British Columbia. In company with the Rev. Henry Horlock, Norman Lee left England from Liverpool in April 1882 on the S.S. *Servia*, bound for New York. After a six-day train journey from there, they arrived in San Francisco, had a rest and saw the sights.

Together the two left for British Columbia. At Yale, where they met disillusioned prospectors, Norman's mining fever seems to have been cured, and at Kamloops he worked on a ranch, measured rock on a Canadian Pacific construction crew, and clerked for the

The Baldwin.

San Francisco, Cal. 19th May 1882.

My dear Aunt Maggie,

You will, I am sure, be wondering why you have not heard from me. As I had a lot to do before I left. I thought I would write my letters from Queenstown but by the time I got there, I thought very differently. I hardly got right from sea sickness the whole time. Since then, writing has been impossible. I shall hope to write again when we get safely landed. We are just off now to the ship, once more. This is a very fine town! I did not care for New York at all. The people are as good as their masters. and the air one breathes even seems to be the essence of republicanism. Everybody here (San Fran.) is very civil. — We had rather a time of it 'in the cars'. We were a week coming from N. Y. to here, and had to sleep on our seats the whole time as we went 2nd class. The 'almighty dollar (as Mr. Horlock calls it) is everywhere. Things are a bit cheaper here than in New York. There you had

to pay a dollar (4/2) for having your
hair cut! and in fact for almost
every thing. We met some very
decent people on the 'cars', who
gave us their ideas of things
in general. I always observe
that the people who tell tales
of the money that is to be made
&c &c, and the money they have
made, and spent, are always
pretty threadbare themselves.
I must stop now, as I have
to look after our luggage.
with my best love to all,
ever your affectionate nephew,
Norman. Lee

No blotting paper

Hudson's Bay Company. There in the store he met the people of the district, including H. P. Bayliff, who had worked for Cornwall at Ashcroft and for Roper at Cherry Creek while learning the cattle-ranching business.

In 1886 Bayliff and Lee joined forces, bought breeding stock from Roper and drove them north of the Chilcotin River to bunch grass, plentiful meadows of good wild hay, and willows, which protected the cattle in winter. The men discovered themselves to be a very long way from either neighbours or a market, in an area relentlessly cold in winter, but hot, dry and dusty in summer.

In general, raising cattle at Redstone, a hundred miles east of 150-Mile House and the Cariboo Road, would hardly seem attractive when Norman Lee settled there—"Old Lee" the Indians called him, because he was the first of the family to come.

Norman Lee left Bayliff and Redstone in 1894 and from Ole Norberg at Hanceville bought a log cabin, which he called "Beaver Ranch." There he settled to raise cattle, operate a store and trade in furs. Through the store, the only one between the Fraser River and Bella Coola, he made his living, but not without work and hardship. At times he employed upward of fifty Indians to pack goods and supplies from Ashcroft. Lack of market rather than any loss of interest made his increasing cattle herd seem only secondary at this time, but when he started north on the drive he was once more primarily a cattleman.

On the journey Norman kept a diary and wrote letters. When he returned to Hanceville, broke but not broken, he reconstructed his adventure from the diary and illustrated the story with sketches. He did not write or sketch for publication; he wrote only for himself and for his family. The journal has not been edited in the usual sense; it has merely been made available, in print, in his words. The sketches reproduced here are those of the original. Where necessary, present-day spellings of proper names have been indicated on their first appearance; standardized orthography for some names had not yet been established when he wrote. In this printed version of his journal, for increased ease in reading, the ampersands have been replaced, the punctuation has been defined, and paragraph divisions have been indicated.

This journal and the letters show Lee's aims, his problems and his disappointments, but also his views on such topics as preachers, Indian relics, Robert-the-dog, and government bungling; they mention some of the people he met, and some of whom he only heard. Sir Arthur Curtis of Hampshire, for example, had been going to the Yukon with a man called Pocock, but on June 10, 1898, had disappeared in the vicinity of Mud River while searching for five strayed horses. Senator Reid's bill and Norman Lee's reply to it suggest what happens, even in the hinterland, when two men of intelligence and wit meet. The journal shows a man who courageously gambled his cattle and lost his fortune, but not his sense of humour. That the drive was unsuccessful matters little to a reader today. In fact, its being unsuccessful gave "Old Lee" the Stikine-to-Wrangell episode to relate, as well as the experience of borrowing money on his arrival in Vancouver.

After travelling from the coast to Ashcroft by train and from there to Hanceville on a horse borrowed from F. A. "Doc" English, Norman Lee again began as cattleman and merchant. In 1902 he visited England and married his second cousin, Agnes "Nessie" Lee, third daughter of William Henry and Agnes Lee of Oakhurst. In 1905 they brought Dan, an adopted son, to the Chilcotin, During the First World War, Norman left the ranch and joined the Gordon Highlanders, but at the age of 52 could not go overseas; Mrs. Lee then lived in Victoria.

Over the 20 years following the war's end, Norman Lee became a legend. As the years wore on, this kind and generous man withered somewhat, but his eyes glittered more than ever from out of the wrinkles above his neatly trimmed moustache; he had time to become more and more interested in the world about him. Life was easier on the ranch by that time: roads were improved, communication was better, neighbours were less distant. The new Pacific Great Eastern Railway allowed the shipment of his purebred Herefords from Williams Lake and made unnecessary the long drives to Ashcroft. New immigrants always recall his friendliness; Indians repaid his decency with loyalty. For everyone he had a nickname that stuck like a burr—"Fatty" he always called the Edward Durban Sheringham mentioned in the journal. Every two weeks or so each summer, Norman Lee rattled at breakneck speed across Becher's Prairie, taking some holidaying youngster from Williams Lake to the ranch. There they rode the range, fished in the nearby Chilcotin River and swam behind the log dam below the house.

Norman Lee died on March 16, 1939, at the age of 77, his wife Agnes in December 1958, his sister Helen in 1954. Dan and his wife Margaret now own the ranch; "Young Lee," or "E. P.," as Edward Penrose was known, still lives at Redstone. "Old Lee" left a legend that lives on, a legend substantiated by this journal and by men like his driver and scow captain, William Copeland. He wrote in 1958 that he had never known a better boss than Norman Lee, who was "more like a brother" and always "honest about what he wanted and what he said."

Gordon R. Elliott
Vancouver, British Columbia, 1960

LETTER TO HIS SISTER GRACE

Chilcotin, B.C.
1st April '98

My dearest Gee.

I really think I shall have to take the beef north this summer. It seems to be the chance of a lifetime to make a few dollars. I do not see much chance to lose anything, and one may make a good deal, so that I am afraid I shall have to keep you waiting till I get back, and then I shall have lots of money and we will go on the spree. In the meantime keep your spirits up, and I will promise faithfully to come over when I get back if I have to steal money to buy a ticket. We shall probably start about the middle of May, when the grass is good, and it will take about three months to get there.

There is a great crowd of people going all the time, so I do not see how they can fail to want beef. I shall probably drive about 200 head, and will take about six men. We shall also have to take quite a pack train to pack grub. We intend to take shot guns and rifles and I expect to have a good time. I think we will get rather sick of cows in three months as one cannot go more than 10 or 12 miles a day as the brutes would get poor.

I do not know how long it will take to get rid of the beef, but will try and dispose of them as soon as possible, as I don't want to get stuck in that country in the winter. It is just possible that I may not go—if I hear anything very discouraging, but the way things look just now it seems a chance not to be missed.

If you write when you get this it will catch me before I start. Later on I will give you another address. Thanks for books &c that you sent. The one of Nellie's was very amusing. Mrs. Gorden seems to be failing. She sends me cards almost every week.

I think we are going to have good times in this country for the next few years. There is actually a demand for beef, and prices are looking up. No more at present as I expect the mail man.

With much love,
your ever attached,
N. L.

The last cattle drive from Hanceville heads for Ashcroft in 1912

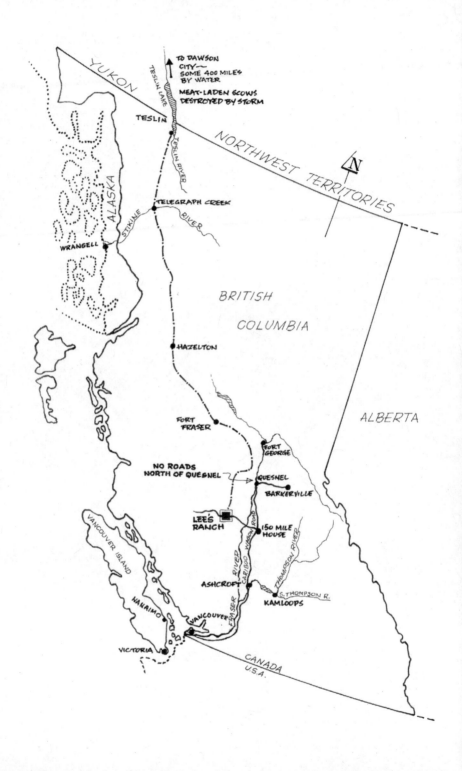

Hanceville
17th May, 1898

We started out gaily enough on the seventeenth of May with about two hundred head of beef cattle. The packtrain of nine horses had gone ahead in charge of two men (one to attend to the horses, and the other to cook for the crowd). The cook of course took the lead, the boss packer bringing up the rear. Five men besides myself drove the cattle. We had concluded to try an unknown road down the Blackwater [West Road] which was supposed to shorten the distance. The first night from home we camped on the Anaham [Anahim] flat. The cattle all being fresh had to be night herded; which in a pouring rain is the reverse of pleasant. From there we moved to Young's place where we had to lay over a day as some of the horses proved to be unsuitable.

For the next few days nothing of any importance took place. Feed was not good—which told on the horses, especially as they were worked pretty hard at the start. Our cook Tabby surprised us by becoming sick and unable to work. We all thought he was shamming, so did not pay much attention to him, except to appoint one of our Indians to cook instead. We found on the whole pretty good camps along the Blackwater, and jogged along at the rate of 10 or 12 miles a day. The cattle were hard to drive as the trail, not being much used, was frequently covered with fallen timber so that our horses got pretty well used up chasing them back to the band whenever they would break away.

About a hundred miles from here we camped for the night where an Indian had fenced in some kind of a ranch. He was an educated genius who kept a kind of store and sold pipes, jack knives, &c. to the other Indians. I also incidentally discovered that he sold rum. From this place to the main Telegraph trail, the trail was so little used that I was obliged to hire an Indian to show us the way. [From Chilcotin, drives could meet the old Telegraph trail constructed between 1865–67 by the Collins Overland Telegraph which was trying to build a line from New York to London by way of Siberia. The slashing had been completed from Quesnel to Telegraph Creek, but by 1898 would be of questionable character.] He only had one eye, but was one of the best men to find the cattle by following up their tracks that I have ever seen. All through this country the timber is thick so that when the cattle got scattered at night it was sometimes quite an art to find them again.

On Sunday the 29th of May we arrived at a river of considerable size. We had been told that this would be very bad to cross but managed to get over without much trouble. All the next day we travelled through timber without a sign of anything for the cattle to eat, but just as we were despairing of finding a camping ground, we came on an opening of a hundred acres or so. Much to our disgust we found that an Indian had fenced it in, and would no doubt charge us much money for the privilege of putting the cattle inside the fence. On investigating, however, we were pleased to find that the proprietor was not at home, so that in a short while, the cattle were safely fenced in for the night. [This] was one of our best camps, as thanks to the fence-building native, we had a rest from night herding.

LETTER TO HIS SISTER GRACE

Hanceville, P.O.
18th May '98

Dear Gee.

Just a line to let you know that the cattle are on the road and that I leave myself tomorrow. I can not write much as I have had a bad dose of sore eyes (for the first time in my existence). I am beginning to funk the trip a good deal as the mosquitoes and flies and things will be awful, to say nothing of the chance of coming out behind. However I am in for it now.

I have written Murray instructing him to pay your div. out of Nellie's & P's money till I come back, so that you will be sure of that for a while.

Send a line to
    c/o John Calbreath
    Telegraph Creek
    B. C.

but don't send many as they may miss fire. Please let Whelk have the address & tell her that I am off. I have to write a good deal and want to save my eyes or would send her a line.

Salute the brethren. Take care of yourself, old fellow. I have just got your last letter. Will come over if I can get away (and exist) and have any money next winter.

Ta ta
Adios.
N. L.

I met the Indian on the trail several days afterwards, and of course the Indian who was working for me told him how we had camped on his ground. He rode up to me looking very fierce, and wanted to know what I meant by it. I meekly tried to explain that there was no other place to camp, but he didn't see the point of the joke and said, "Suppose I stop I take your money." How I rejoiced that he hadn't "stopped." So I told him with a smile that I did not try to conceal, "I think more better you no stop ain't it?" He looked very sour, but realizing that it was rather late in the day to protest, moved on.

The next day we came early to some more water which had to be crossed. It was only about forty feet across, but was deep enough to make the cattle swim. The trail was hedged in with bushes so that the animals could not see the way out on the other side and absolutely refused to go across. We had to cut a trail round (some 5 or 6 miles) to find a better crossing, and it was night when we at length reached the other side. Two days more took us to the Telegraph trail about fifty miles from Quesnelle [Quesnel].

So far we had been travelling alone, but now that we were on the main road to the golden north, we were surprised to see the crowds of pilgrims flocking north. Every half hour, one or more packtrains would go on up the trail. All kinds and varieties of horses, all sorts and conditions of men. They were evidently prepared for war, as hardly a man passed but was hung all over with six shooters and bowie knives. The trail was much better than we had had before, being cut out eight feet wide and as straight as an arrow for miles. It was a pretty sight to see the cattle along this trail stringing out one behind the other with a cowpuncher behind every thirty or forty (see picture).

At the end of the first day on this trail we camped at Mud River, a small river which however seemed to be deep enough to require swimming: An Indian had built a raft and was busily engaged ferrying people, horses, and goods across. He must have coined money as his charges were pretty stiff. I made a bargain with him to cross my stuff and then I made a discovery. A little way down the stream was a trail leading to the river which I followed and found that I could ford the cattle and pack animals easily, which was duly done, and our example was followed by all the other pilgrims who were about to cross with the help of the Indian. The ferryman saw that his business was at an end, so climbing onto his raft, he got up steam and vanished down the creek. Later on we discovered the reason of things. It appeared that the river was fordable except at high water, but Mister Indian thought it was a good chance to make a little out of the white man, so he took his axe and proceeded to throw trees across the stream down below out of sight, thereby backing up the water, and making a very pretty chance to do ferry business. A short while before we came along, someone who knew the ways of the river, being surprised at the depth of water, looked up and down and discovered the fraud. It was at this place that Sir Arthur Curtis was lost and never heard of again, some few days after we had passed. The horses strayed here and we were glad when we were able to get away after being delayed for a day or two hunting them.

At this place one of my Indians started for home and I thought it well to send Tabby back too. We had thought that he had been shamming sick, but at

Telegraph trail cattle stringing along. Pine trees at each side cow punchers between cattle

last began to think it was getting serious as he used to swell much all over, and his face turned blue! We were somewhat shorthanded for a while after this, and to add to our troubles, the cook refused to cook any more. I tried one after another the other members of the party but none of them wanted to cook, which very nearly decided me on turning homewards, as I did not propose to cook myself. However just in the nick of time along came two fellows looking for a job. Two great big Missourians [sic] of course hung about with the inevitable six shooters and bowie knives (see pictures). I said I would give them both a job if one would cook, but they didn't care for cookery and went away. Next day they were back again, ready to work if I would give the cook a little more pay, which I was glad enough to do.

Phil took charge of the packtrain and Jake tried to cook. He was willing but he was not a cook. He tormented us for some 300 miles. I was frequently so blind and dizzy with that grand American complaint "Dispepsy" that I couldn't count the cattle properly. One Jack Macauly of Chilcoten [Chilcotin] camped with us one evening. I asked him what he thought of our cook. He said, "I don't call him a cook at all, he's a *flure* destroyer," and he was!

About 125 miles from Quesnelle we came to Tsincut [Sinkut] Lake where [there] was good feed for the animals. A small stream came out of the lake, which was deep enough to make animals swim. There was however no ferryman here and the reason

6

was explained. When one came to the stream a good ford was found by keeping well out into the lake, where one would hardly expect to find a ford. An Indian taking in this situation had cut a good wide trail to the stream, as shown by the dotted lines, with a fine trail on the other side also, making it appear as if one must swim

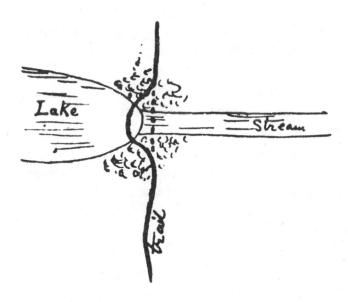

one's animals across the stream. He then built a raft and made much money crossing people and baggage, while all the time there was a good ford a few yards off. Happily the fraud was discovered a few days before our party came along. Six miles more took us to some fine open range close to Stoney [Stony] Creek. Here we hung up for three days to give our horses and cattle a much needed rest. We killed a small heifer and had plenty of fresh beef for a change, and sold some to the pilgrims who passed by.

Of the cattle that started from Chilcoten, Jim Cornell was about a week ahead of us with seventy five head, Jerry Gravelle about three days with one hundred, and we heard that Johnny Harris with his two hundred was trying hard to catch us up. About this time we fell in with a party from Montreal who had started with their pack-train from the American side. I saw a good deal of these people at one time and another and was favourably impressed by them. Here for the first time we came across the "Burro" outfit—a packtrain of forty or fifty little mokes, which their owners expected to make lots of money out of when they reached the north. The poor little donks however were a failure. Used to a rocky dry country, they could not stand the mud and wet weather which began to make an appearance, and wherever there was a swampy bit of road the owners had great difficulty to get them to move. I saw one man between sixty and seventy years of age armed with a heavy club, whacking away at the ears of the wretched beasts, saying, "You appear to like it, take lots of it!" The poor little rabbits looked so innocent with great big staring eyes and ears a foot and a half long.

There is a large rancherie at Stoney Creek, and as we heard the Indians were to have a *danse* all the pilgrims who were camped in the neighborhood went to see the fun. It turned out to be the usual very tame affair. One savage scraped the same old tune again and again on an ancient fiddle while some of the young braves took turns at step dancing. The women were conspicuous by their absence. The monotony was enlivened when a quadrille was got up by the whites, who at any rate made plenty of noise with their heavy boots. The Indians thought the exhibition was fine, and called lustily for "eight white man one more time."

On the afternoon of our last day at Stoney Creek—I think I mentioned that we stayed there three days—Harris passed us with his band of 200 cattle. As he had purchased his stock in Chilcoten, I took the opportunity of looking through his band, and found one of my own steers. This I tried to induce Harris to hand over at once, but he declined, saying that he had bought and paid for it. My men

McKeo going into cattle at Mudhole.

were all in readiness to take the animal forcibly, but on consideration, I thought the best course would be to go for the man who had sold the steer, especially as Harris's men were quite ready for the fray and they appeared to be a stouter lot of men than mine, though my outfit were better mounted. Harris camped that night three or four miles further on.

Next day we pulled out again, the animals having picked up wonderfully in the three days, and by noon of the second day reached the Nechaco [Nechako] River, the first of the three great streams that we had to cross. Leaving the cattle and going on ahead to the ferry, I found that Harris had not yet got all his cattle across, having had considerable difficulty in swimming them. Two or three had got lost in the brush, so that we had to camp for the night in order to let him get out of our way.

Next day we drove to the river and made a very successful crossing. The stream divided above the ferry, which gave the ferryman

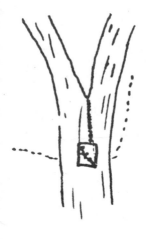

a chance to fasten his scow to the point of land between the two streams by a long cable, and by moving the scow to catch the current of the river, it was made to run back and forwards at will. I found that the ferryman was not grasping, as he let me off with $12.00 for crossing all the horses and men, and helping to swim the cattle. We camped for the night across the river, where we found a rancherie and Hudson's Bay Post known as Frazer [Fraser] Lake Post.

Fortunately we did not have to purchase much here, as prices were high. Flour $7.00 a bag and so forth. The man in charge of the Post looked as if he were getting old before his time. He was apparently the only white man in that section of the country. We asked him how often he got his mail in that lonely spot, to which he replied, "We never get any mail here!" What a life!

As Harris was still bungling at the river, we pulled out the next day before him, but before we had gone many miles, it turned out that he preferred losing a steer or two to staying behind. He accordingly started off his packtrain, which overtook our cattle and forced its way through the band, scattering the cattle into the woods. One reason for the haste was that Harris, having been packing for years on this trail as far as Hazleton [Hazelton], knew the good camping places; so that he sent his packtrain ahead of our cattle to secure a good camp ground for the night. For two or three days I was annoyed by Harris and his packtrain, and at last determined to let him pass again in order to be rid of him. About this stage of the drive I thought I was rather cute to travel easily and keep the animals in good condition. After Harris had passed again, he slackened his pace, and I was kept waiting several times by finding his cattle in the way.

From Frazer Lake almost to Hazleton we had fine feed for the stock. The country is heavily timbered (mostly with cottonwood) all the way, but every two or three miles one would come to openings of from 10 to 2 or 300 acres of fine feed. We had no more night herding to do, as the stock hardly scattered at all. The feed was so good, and for several weeks we had quite a pleasant time.

In the morning we would start off with the cattle before the sun got strong, leaving the packtrain to follow us as soon as they had loaded up. The Indian Billy drove the spare saddle horses ahead of the cattle, and about noon would hunt up a good feeding ground, build a fire, and have a lunch and cup of tea ready for us when we came along. We would bask in the sun for an hour or two while the cattle lay down all round, too full to move. Then our packtrain and cook would pass us, and after leaving our marks on a tree or two, we would start again for the afternoon drive, and find the tents all pitched and the season's delicacies spread out ready for us when evening came, by Jake and Phil.

Some distance from Frazer Lake we got into a "Poisonous" country. The first intimation we had of it was that one place at which we camped was generally known as "Poison Flat." Why, we did not know, but found out in a day or two. On leaving Poison Flat in the morning I counted the cattle and made one short. Counted again, and still one short. Now when cattle were missing out of the band one would never go alone, always two or three or more, so, thinking I must have made a mistake in the count, I started the cattle off. On getting into camp at night, I counted again, and still one short.

Next day we rested, and Sheringham and I went back to look for the missing animal and found him at Poison Flat, a fine 3 yr old steer, on his back with his heels in the air, a victim to Poisonous weed. This weed is described as being a small blue flower called wild Larkspur, of which the root is said to be poisonous.

This steer was our first loss since leaving home, which we thought pretty good, as Harris had already lost some 12 or 15. As he had advised us to camp at this place, we were not altogether sorry to notice that one of his steers had turned up its toes at the place where he camped some three miles further on. For several days after leaving this place, cattle would sicken and fall out of the band as we were driving along, and we would give them up for lost; but they always recovered and came trotting along behind after a while. We heard afterwards that the proper course was to bleed them by chopping off a piece of their tails and feed them much bacon grease.

We were annoyed slightly at times by Indians, who would put a useless fence round a little piece of hay ground, and then want to charge us much money because the cattle broke through the fence. "Mac" settled all difficulties however one day by giving an Indian a businesslike kick on the usual place, so that they bothered us no more.

About half way between Frazer Lake and Hazleton, we came to a house owned by Siwashes. The proprietor was on the trail waylaying the pilgrims. He stated that the government trail was very bad going, and that he himself had cut out another trail, a distance of some thirty miles, which was much better. On the strength of his work, he coaxed and bullied money out of the travellers. I told him, as he said he was going to Hazleton, that I might give him something when I arrived there, if I saw fit. I did not see fit. Almost all the pilgrims took the new trail and found it much worse than the

government trail, and 12 or 15 miles further. We got onto the government trail again about 100 miles from Hazleton.

About the same time that the rush of miners began from Quesnelle, our intelligent government sent out a party of men to put the trail in good condition. The men were hired at Quesnelle, but instead of starting to work from there, they were sent through to Hazleton, and made to work back from that point to Quesnelle. The consequence was that most of the travel was over by the time the trail party began to work back, so that while we had to wallow last year through mud and swamps, there is now a fine trail with good bridges which cost the gov^t lots of money but which was finished too late to be of any use except to an occasional Indian, as I may safely say that the bridges will have rotted before such another insane rush takes place over the Telegraph trail.

On the 6th of July we arrived at Mauricetown [Moricetown] a place of which we had heard a good deal. It turned out to be an Indian Village about thirty miles from Hazleton, on the Bulkley River, a stream of considerable size which flows into the Skeena at

Hazleton. The river at this point passes between two rocks, and is easily spanned by a crazy bridge, after falling some twenty or thirty feet. All about the canyon through which the river was boiling and dashing, the Indians had rigged ingenious platforms, with rope made of willow roots, from which they speared salmon, and caught them in dip nets. It appeared to be extremely dangerous work, especially for small children who could scarcely lift a salmon from the water when caught. The chances of anyone getting out of the boiling cauldron alive, if they should happen to fall in, were very slight, but we were told that no accidents had ever taken place. After a long diet of bacon, it was a treat to get a few fresh salmon, and some potatoes which I procured from the Indians. Though only 30 miles from Hazleton the Indians here cannot understand those from that place, and a few miles from Hazleton is another Indian settlement with still another entirely different language. I should very much have liked to procure a photograph of Mauricetown, and may perhaps do so yet.

We were bothered a good deal by our packtrain men not being able to judge what should be a good day's travel. Arriving at Mauricetown in the evening with tired cattle, we found that the packtrain with our supper and blankets had gone further on. As it was impossible for us to go further, we were obliged to accept the hospitality of two of the pilgrims who were camped there. It turned out later that the packtrain had travelled that day thirty miles, whereas our usual march was ten or twelve. We did not catch the train for two days.

From Mauricetown to Hazleton we found the feed getting very poor, the country being thickly covered with brush and hazel bushes, which in places almost covered the trail in. Over "Bear River" 12 miles from Hazleton was an extremely crazy bridge built of two or three logs. We preferred swimming the cattle. We had been in

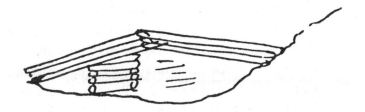

fear of Bear River ever since leaving home, as we were told that it would often rise in a night so as to be impassable, but on this occasion it was kind.

The next day we camped four miles from Hazleton, where we found quite a town of tents—most of the people who had passed us on the trail. Some were resting their animals while they procured more provisions at Hazleton, others were dissolving partnership and selling out their possessions, with a view to taking the steamer down the river for home. A great many were scared by reason of the tales told of the want of feed further on. Going down to the town, I was just in time to see the steamer owned by the H . B. Co. coming up the Skeena River with supplies. We were told that this steamer usually makes two runs in a year from the coast.

Hazleton is an extremely one horse place consisting chiefly of the Hudson's Bay Co.'s store, and another store, an Indian Agent's residence, and an English church mission of sorts. The size of the town is increased by Indian houses wedged in among those of the whites. Here we got our first sight of Totem poles, placed in front of the Indians' houses, some of which were said to be many hundreds of years old. The most curious feature of the place is the Indian burying ground. I have seen nothing to equal it in the country. Little buildings, like summer houses, were placed over the graves, many very neatly built, with doors and windows. In these buildings were placed all manner of things belonging to the deceased.

The most splendid of the lot was furnished complete with a carpet, table, chairs, washbasin &c., two new umbrellas, and a whole assortment of new shawls, blankets and all manner of nameless lady's properties, not to mention a full sized portrait of the tenant in a massive frame. I tried to induce my Indian Billy to look at the show through one of the windows, but his superstitions stood in his way. Even the poorest of the graves had one or two large trunks, apparently filled with the deceased's property.

I intended resting the animals at Hazleton for three days, and took the packtrain down to town for a new store of food which I procured at the Hudson Bay Store. The stores were doing a great business by reason of the unusual travel. I was able to work off a few cattle to the Hudson Bay man, which saved me from paying him much money. When I was nearly ready to leave town again the Indian Billy determined to return home, and Mac also left me, saying that he would prefer to push ahead quicker. Having to get two more men in a hurry, I took the first two that offered, one of whom took the undesirable job of cooking. We thought at first that he was a pretty good cook, as he fed us on "slapjacks," which were good for a change, but by the time he fed us on slapjacks all the way from Hazleton to Telegraph Creek, we became heartily sick of that form of diet, not to say dyspeptic. When the third day of our stay at Hazleton had reached its close, I was all ready to pull out again, but the next day my cowboys saw fit to indulge in an excess of Hudson Bay Rum, and were consequently useless. The next day they were undergoing the sobering up process, and were more useless still.

So on the sixth day we started and reached the crossing of the Skeena River, at the Kispiox Rancherie, some seven miles up the river from Hazleton. Next day we were ready to tackle the river, but could not round up all the cattle. The next morning we halloed across the river to the Indians, but there was no response till an hour or two afterwards when we realized the reason by the jingling of a tin kettle church bell. These Indians were Methodists and would do no work on Sunday, unless they could do it without being found out; so there was no crossing that day. Next morning the Indians were over betimes, but it was twelve o'clock before the crossing began. The bargaining process had first to be undergone. They flatly refused to cross me for less than 85 dollars. After much debate I got them down to sixty, and I am happy to say they earned every cent of it. The cattle did not want to swim, and it took twenty-five or thirty Indians and five canoes all that day and the next as well to get the animals over. We just got the last beast across by sundown on the second day. The river was very high and proved to be a hard swim for the cattle and horses.

We were obliged to camp in the rancherie that night which was composed of neatly built houses that would have been a credit to a "white" town in B.C. There were a few tumble-down old shacks with more "Totem poles," but these, we were told, belonged to the heathen. (Reflections on the advantages of being a Methodist Indian.) I never experienced before to such an extent the native dog. Here and at Hazleton were dogs everywhere. Each family seemed to own up to forty or fifty of the hungriest curs it is possible to imagine. Many of the Indians at this time of the year were down at the coast working for the salmon canneries, consequently their dogs were left behind to do the best they could for themselves, and they certainly lost no opportunity. Anything in the eatable line had to be most carefully watched. I have seen a dozen or so watching a pilgrim frying his bacon, and the instant his back was turned they would grab the scalding mess out of the frying pan, when still on the fire. (Imaginary picture of these brutes, which I wish I had.)

We were glad to leave this rancherie, but were delayed another half day, by failing to find Sheringham's horse. We concluded at last

17

no feed O 18 m. no feed X 17 miles good feed along here X

20 m.

small miles little feed flat

O Some feed on mountain

18 miles

O small march little feed.

8 hours

O good feed large meadow

10 m. 2 feet

O small lake, a little grass.

20 miles X 20 miles no feed

20 miles ... good feed

X Skeena river

O Hazleton

that the Indians must have stolen it, as it was fat like its owner, and as time was becoming precious [we] had to leave without finding it. For about twelve miles after crossing the river we had abundance of good feed.

I should have mentioned, before bidding adieu to Hazleton, that we found there a man who knew something of the trail ahead of us. Another party had been despatched by the Government to clear the trail from Hazleton to Telegraph Creek, and this man had worked with the party some hundred and eighty miles, had there left them and returned to Hazelton. He made a rough sketch of the trail and nailed it up on the door of his cabin, for the benefit of the pilgrims. Said sketch I now reproduce. Not a very promising outlook to people who could only travel about ten miles a day.

Some people gave up the attempt after seeing this sketch, but the majority thought they could go where others had gone, and every one agreed that the road maker must be a prevaricator. The Summit was said to be

18

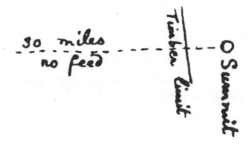

about 180 miles from Hazleton, and as all the Government and other reports agreed that it was only 200 miles to Telegraph Creek, it appeared that one only had to drop down from the "Summit" to be right in town.

We had now arrived at the end of feed, and started out to negotiate the "no feed" country. We could hardly have imagined a country with absolutely no picking of any kind, but here it was. For about 10 miles we travelled through desolation. Hemlock timber always, varied occasionally by Alder brush and Devil's clubs, a species of weed properly named, an inch or more in diameter, covered with prickles, which twists and twines among the fallen timber which of course is everywhere. At night nothing for the animals to eat; all hands turned to and built a corral to hold the cattle while the horses were tied to trees. By morning we had found a handful or two of grass for the horses, and started for the next run. By evening we arrived at "Small Lake little grass." The road man had not lied.

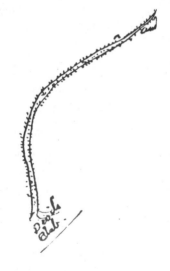

Imagine about an acre of swamp on which four hundred head of cattle had already camped, not to mention almost all the pack animals that had gone up the road as well. But there was no help for it so we turned the cattle loose to try and pick up a mouthful and sat down to wait for the packtrain, and the man with the lunch who had not yet turned up. They did not turn up. Fortunately there were other campers at this place who took pity on us and fed us. We did not need blankets, as we had to trudge round the swamp all night in the rain holding the cattle. N.B. It had rained hard every day since we left Hazleton. Will Copeland and I snatched a little sleep in an inch or two of water on the swamp, but the others failed to find any.

We could not stay here to wait for the packtrain so pulled out, after leaving messages on the trees for those behind, who of course failed to find them. By night, after travelling through country quite as bad as that of the day before, and wading through mud almost all the way, we arrived at "good feed, large meadow."

This was a fairly large opening, and there was still some feed on it. A large number of pilgrims were camped here, resting their animals, which was fortunate for us as there was still no packtrain. We divided ourselves up among the campers, who treated us very well. At 10 o'clock at night the loose horse driver turned up with one loose horse. The others he had more or less lost and had left them in the timber. The packtrain was said to be advancing slowly through the mud.

Wed 27th July. Started two men back to look for packtrain. They do not return.

Thursday 28. Count cattle, five short. Do not dare to ride for fear of playing out horses. No rain today. Packtrain turns up at night with only half the load, having had an awful time through the mud, having left two horses (played out) on the road.

Friday 29. Rest all animals.

LETTER TO HIS SISTER HELEN

Hazleton on the Skeena River
Sometime about the 14th of July.

Have got this far at last and have been stopping here for three or four days getting supplies. This is a town about the size of Ashcroft, a secluded spot. The steam boat gets here from the world outside three times in a year, so that the news is not of the latest. It just happened to get in when I arrived and went out again at once. Several people were going down on her so that I just had time to address an envelope, put a stone in it and hurl it onto the boat, with a request to a nice young man to send a line. I didn't find out his name. If he writes you might let me know it. It appears the boat is to make an extraordinary effort and come again in a week, hence this. We have had pretty good luck so far. One passes through a country where there is a poisoned weed which kills cattle. We lost one. Another fellow ahead of us one. Some men behind lost two. There are crowds of pilgrims going up the trail. Mostly Americans. Some of them hung all over with knives and six shooters. They are all sorry they have come this way, as it takes such a time to get anywhere. We have just been going two months now. I will try and send a better yarn from Glenora. At present have not time for much. We have met some very decent fellows along the road. Most all the parties split up sooner or later—get to wrangling. I think we are about the only crowd that gets along all right. I have been short handed several times as some of the fellows have left and gone ahead, but I have now got the right number. One gets a trifle tired of cattle sometimes. They are "real" mean to drive now and then. I don't know how it is going to turn out about the sale of the cattle. We do not hear very encouraging reports, but no one knows much more than we do. I am afraid I shall have to take the beef right through to Dawson which will probably run me further into the winter than I want to stay in that filthy country, but we are in for it now and will have to stay with it till we are rid of the beef. I will send you a line from Glenora.

till then "adieu."
salute the brethren
& be good to yourselves.
Ta ta
N. L.

Send this on to G.A.L.

Sat^y 30. Send packtrain back and get rest of load.

Sunday 31. Rest, and boil clothes.—It was almost impossible to wash our clothes usually, as we had no time, and no receptacle large enough to cook them in.—Nothing short of boiling was of any use.

We now concluded to drive the cattle in future on foot in order to give the horses every chance. We also now perceived the mistake of having allowed Harris and the other cattle men to get ahead of us, as the trail almost all the way was a sea of mud—such as I have never seen before. Whenever animals moved down a hill the mud rolled down too after the manner of a river, thick pasty mud about the consistency of porridge. It was now borne in upon us that horses were getting weak. This would have been a nice point to have turned back from, but we did not turn back. We threw away now everything that was not necessary. Shotgun, shovels, picks, one fine large tent—even two gold pans to lighten the load. The hobbles that we had used to restrain the horses—I burnt; about a dozen pair, in order to be certain that they would be used no more. The packtrain man, Phil, was too fond of hobbling the horses so that they would not stray far away, but which had the effect of thinning them considerably.

Monday Augt 1. Started again and travelled 15 miles—good camp but eaten out. Will Copeland left the last of his two horses beside the trail to die, having thrown away his saddle.

Tues. 2. Reach "small marsh little feed," smile at it and pass on. Send Sheringham on ahead to locate camping ground. He goes too far, we see him no more, at night reach a corral built by Harris and put cattle therein. A notice on a tree says, "Good feed—follow up creek." Of course where Harris had been was eaten off, but further on, we found a meadow that he had not reached, where the feed was good.

Wed. 3. One steer short. Cattle go on, Elliot and I go back and find missing steer and two more belonging to Harris, corral them, and sleep *sans* grub or blankets.

Thurs. 4. Up early and overtake cattle at "Steelyard" camp. Steelyard camp was so named from the fact that at this place I parted with everything that had not already been thrown aside, with the exception of food and blankets; among other things one Steelyard, which I had stayed with in the hope of using it some day to weigh beef on. The instrument was suspended, nicely balanced, from a tripod, and all the rest of the stuff put into a sack, and hung therefrom.

By this time we were in the thick of the misery—as regards mud and shortness of feed. For some time there had been no spare horses to drive, as every horse was used for packing, not that there was much to pack, but that the animals had become so weak as to be hardly capable of carrying more than a saddle. Every day one or more of our horses had to be left beside the trail, and not ours alone, as it was scarce possible to travel a hundred yards without finding dead or abandoned horses; I have seen in one place two dead horses on each side of the trail. The poor little burros especially could not stand the mud. Of the packtrain of fifty or sixty pretty nearly all died or had to be left. The mud seemed to make horses' legs sore. Some people claimed that they got poisoned, every one knew they were starved. A horse would get a small sore on his hoof or leg, which would never get better, but rather worse with every knock, until in a few days he would

23

become dead lame, and had to be left behind. Happy the horse whose owner possessed a pistol, at the moment of parting. Many were left without a bite to eat, and a notice on a tree, "If my horse is fit to travel, bring him along." Very few were ever brought along. We were not the only ones who threw things away, as the trail was covered with coils of rope, boxes of candles, matches, anything—to say nothing of scores of riding and pack saddles. There were three good stock saddles left at one of my camps.

Very few of the pilgrims rode horses now. Everyone had to foot it through the mud. Almost every day the trail was one succession of mud and swamps from one end to the other. There had been no attempt at making a trail, beyond what little chopping was actually necessary to get animals through. Whether the road party had originally intended to make a good trail, I know not. As soon as they left Hazleton, they were followed at once by crowds of prospectors, who would urge them on, so that all they could do was to keep out of the way of those behind. Up and down the most ridiculous mountains, through mud all the way. If they went in the wrong direction, they had no time to retrace their steps but kept going, with all the other idiots behind them. One day we were travelling with the cattle strung out one behind the other for nearly a mile. The men driving the leaders found that the tail end of the procession was only about thirty yards off. The road men had made a trifling bend.

Thursday Aug. 4. Poke along 8 miles. My horse down in slippery creek. Hard to get up.

Friday 5. Packtrain got crazy and went 15 miles. They play out one of the best pack horses. Crossing a crazy bridge broke the leg of one fine steer. Had to leave him without taking a bite.

Tuesday 9. Some cattle missing, 2 men have to go back to look, while the rest move on.

Sat^y 13. Find cattle late, leave at noon. Reach camp at 8.30 pm. All animals tired out. Put cattle in corral built by Harris. No feed at all.

Monday 15 Aug. Reach the Summit (mentioned already) last three miles hard up hill. This summit was known as "groundhog" mountain. As most of the travellers had only laid in grub for two hundred miles, many of them were glad to eat groundhog. We rested here a day or so, as there was some grass, and ate groundhog. For the last week one or two of the boys had been back on the trail looking for missing cattle. A good man was necessary for this job, as he not only had to walk double or treble distance, but find the cattle as well. When I sent the wrong man back one time, three head failed to appear on his return. My big horse very sick. Feed him "bacon grease" which seemed to help him a little.

Thursday 18. Had to kill a three year old steer that was lame. Was able to carry off a quarter of it, gave half away, and traded the other quarter for half a bag of flour.

Monday 22. Through beautiful open valley, lots of feed for two or three days. Too late to be much good to horses. Numbers of ptarmigan, at which the cowboys emptied their pistols. Bill Copeland, however, armed with "clubs" getting the game. We were travelling now at a high altitude, almost to snow line in places, and had to cross many glacier streams over which there was no pretense at a bridge. As we were all on foot, we had to take the streams as they came; some we found swift, and all very cold.

By this time (Thursday 25th Aug^t) we were about two hundred and sixty miles from Hazleton, and I concluded to leave the cattle in order to hasten to Telegraph Creek to see what to do next. The horses had ceased to die now, but were all very weak and sick, so it was out of the question to ride.

Friday Aug, 26. I started out on foot for Telegraph Creek, leaving the cattle to follow. By this time food was getting very scarce, so that I did not care to take much away from the cowpunchers; furthermore, I did not want to carry much. My outfit consisted of three pounds of rice, one spoon, one cup, and a little extract of beef, also 2 single blankets. Not being used to packing on my back, I shed the two blankets in a day or two, as I found I could make better time without them. It turned out later that the distance from where I left the cattle to Telegraph Creek was about 130 miles.

Every day now, I overtook pilgrims who were slowly poking along, very short of grub, and with hardly a horse left. As I knew most of them, I did not have to depend entirely on my rice diet, for which I was thankful (I don't recommend it) and there was usually a blanket to crawl into at night. At the Lepann [Klappan] river (80 miles from T. C.) were two men selling grub. They had originally come out to meet the Curtis party (having come up the coast by steamer) but getting tired of the bad trails were now selling out their flour and bacon at enormous prices to people who came along. Many of the pilgrims had helped to hunt for Sir Arthur Curtis when lost at Mud river, at their own expense for several days, and were not very well pleased to find one of the party waiting here to sell flour to them at seventy five cents a lb., and other things in proportion. I refrained from purchasing and passed on.

Tuesday 30. Overtake Geo. Gafney and Fink, leave them and camp with Paterson the sawmill man, who was coming back to meet his party, with grub. Next day met two more men packing out grub.

Bought 50 lbs flour at 25 cents a pound and a little bacon, cached it at the woods for the cow men blazing a tree with my cow brand, so that the boys would know where to fund the stuff. Fatty, whom I had left in charge of the cattle, could not wait half a day for flour but purchased some more at my expense.

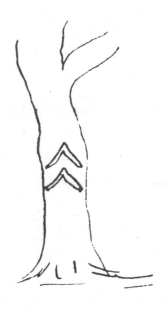

Sept. 1. Fell in with some of Harris's cow men and camped with Harris at night.

Sept. 2. Watch Harris crossing the Stickeen [Stikine], which he does badly. A white man in charge of a ferry boat lays in wait to cross the last of the pilgrims' horses for $ 2.50 per head. Tumble into Telegraph Creek, a miserable one horse place. One or two stores, the inevitable whisky house and a few tents. Find here Jim Cornell, who had arrived one month ahead of me. His band being smaller, and larger sized stock, he was able to make better time. He had started a butcher shop at Telegraph Creek and was getting rid of his beef slowly. He invited me to stop with him and asked me if I wanted any money. I told him he was just the man I wanted to see and would call on him later.

Sat^y Sept. 3. Stayed at T. C. finding things out.

Sunday 4th Septr. Jack McIntosh arrives over the trail. I found that it was impossible to get rid of any quantity of beef at T. C., Glenora, or at Teslin, so saw that the only remaining thing to do was to build scows at Teslin, and take the beef down the river to Dawson. I consequently hired McIntosh to push ahead and see what he could do about getting scows built. I gave him some money (of which I never got any account) with which to buy a pack horse and supplies of oakum, pitch and other necessaries.

Monday 5th Sept. Started back on foot to meet cattle. Nights getting cool for sleeping without blankets.

Tuesday 6. Met cattle.

Wed^y 7. Start Sheringham off to get Indian to cross us (with whom I had made an arrangement). The cattle were badly scattered. It took all day to find them, which upset my arrangements as we could not reach the place to which I had sent on the packtrain. We drove till it got quite dark. No feed for the cattle. Landed them in a lot of fallen timber, and hastily built fires all round the band, in order to hold them together. No supper. Cattle wouldn't lie down. Very restless. All hands had to walk round them all night, one or other of us occasionally snatching a little sleep beside the fire.

Next morning, off again as soon as it was daylight, and reached Harris' camp where we found our packtrain, and had breakfast, after corralling the cattle in a brush corral built by Harris. It was now too late in the day to meet the Indian at the river, which was eight miles from our camp, so we contented ourselves with sleeping and herding the cattle out in the brush to pick up whatever they could. Next day down to the river where made a very successful crossing. The cattle seemed to want to go and gave us very little trouble. My dog took great interest in the crossing, and followed each bunch of cattle over the river, even swimming up stream, and heading off one beast that tried to turn back. The Stickeen is a pretty large river, almost as big as the Frazer.

I had made all arrangements already and had nothing to do but load up some more grub, and start for Teslin; but it was not to be.

Of course some men wanted to quit, others wanted to go to Glenora (twelve miles down the stream) and get boots and shoes and other things. Of course also one or two had to get a full dose of whiskey, so that after the cattle had been lost and found again there were several more valuable days wasted.

At Telegraph Creek and Glenora, we were now on the much advertized "Stickeen route to the Klondyke gold fields." This was to have been the all Canadian route. A railroad was to be built and consequently a wagon road from Glenora to Teslin Lake, where the pilgrims were to take the steamer for Dawson City. Early in March ('98) throngs of people came up the coast in Steamboats to Wrangel [Wrangell], and then began a struggle to get up the Stickeen on the ice. The winter was unusually mild so that the ice was extremely unsafe. The best time to travel was before the sun got up, and after dark. Imagine pulling a hand sleigh loaded with grub through a foot or more of slush, temperature of said slush being at freezing point, often up to the middle in ice cold water, and a keen Northeast wind rushing down the river to meet you.

All kinds of outfits might have been seen. Sleighs pulled by horses, by oxen, by dogs, and by men. Numbers of men and animals were lost in the river. A man would be driving his team with all his worldly possessions on a sleigh. Without any warning, team, sleigh and load would drop through the rotten ice, and the man would be left. Sometimes the man dropped through and the team stayed behind. And yet, after all this misery, if you asked a river pilgrim if he came over the Telegraph trail (the way we came), he would look apologetic and humbly reply, "Oh no, I didn't have it as bad as you, I came up the river on the ice."

And so the rush went on till some of the throng had reached Glenora, and others had to build boats as the ice was breaking up. Some struggled against the stream in all kinds of crazy boats, others who had no boats camped where they were till the steamboats picked them up, which they were in no hurry to do, as they were certain of these passengers, and preferred to load at the coast. Then came a throng of steamboats, several of which were unable to get up the river.

Everything was going to boom. The railroad contractor had already made a start with a wagon road some twenty miles towards Teslin, the Hudson's Bay Company had built a fine large store, everyone was going to make money out of someone else, when the Canadian Senate calmly threw out the railroad bill, and the Stickeen route was knocked cold. To make the failure a complete success, a couple of hundred soldiers were sent through by this route to the Yukon in the early spring. When they arrived at Glenora there were very few pack animals to be had. The smallest kind of a pony fetched some two hundred dollars, and every available steed was pressed into Government service. The consequence was that, pack animals being so scarce, the pilgrims could not get their supplies moved to Teslin Lake for less than forty cents per pound. The majority could not and would not pay this awful price and were consequently brought to a stand at Glenora. Some few stayed there, the larger part took the first steamer down the river for home. There was now no further influx of people up the Stickeen, so that almost all the steamboats betook themselves elsewhere.

We arrived at Telegraph Creek when everything was dead. There was quite a string of determined men pushing their ways towards Teslin Lake. Some started from Glenora with wagons, till they got to the end of the wagon road, and the wagons were then cut down into small carts on which goods were toted along. By the time we arrived horses were more plentiful, and could be bought for from ten to twenty dollars, but such animals. Every bit as bad as those in our train—living corpses. Of course there were lots of them packing goods into Teslin. There were also oxen pulling carts, and packing on their backs. I saw several men wheeling their outfits along on barrows, but would imagine by the time they reached Teslin that they would have eaten all their supplies. I think most of those who came over the Telegraph trail took the first steamer for home, as most of them were "stoney broke," having lost all their horses, and eaten all their provisions.

In consequence of the forty cent a pound freight, I found that I should have to buy more supplies at Glenora, as my pocket would not reach to Teslin Lake prices, so I kept one of my men back, after starting the cattle off, and repaired to Glenora, where I set about picking up another packtrain. I might mention "en passant" that the man that I kept with me was the one that I had hired at Hazleton to drive the loose horses. Of course for a long time there had been no spare horses to drive, but still I kept him. I had heard that he carried no less than 900 dollars in his pocket, and I wanted that nine hundred, or at any rate, a part of it. He also had, at Glenora, about as much more grub as I wanted, which he offered to let me have on the pay-when-you-get-ready plan. I was glad to take the stuff, though I have not "got ready" yet.

With difficulty, I scared up a packtrain of nine half dead animals—sores all over them, and so forth, at about twenty dollars a head—the price somehow always goes up when one wants to buy— loaded up with my pal's grub and made a start for Teslin Lake.

The first day we did about 17 miles and expected to reach town in no time. The next day, horses began to give out, and we had to slow down to 8 or 10 miles. We had fully realized by this time that we must push on as fast as possible if we were to get down the Yukon River, as it was beginning to get cold, but the greater our hurry, the slower got the weary pack animals. Feed was so poor that we had to turn the horses loose at night. On the fourth morning we failed to find three of our best horses. Hunted for them (of course on foot) for two days. There were probably quite a hundred pack animals at that place every night, and I hunted outside of the furthest horse track, old or new, for miles on each side of the camp, and found two of the horses at last within 200 yds of our camp, in a thick clump of brush. The third horse we had to leave, and I sold his load (flour) for two dollars less than I had paid for it—after packing it for four days.

And so we poked slowly along, almost every day a horse giving out and having to be left by the wayside. But we did not part with any more loads. They were too precious. When one horse could not pack any more, his load would have to be divided up among the others.

Tuesday 27th September. Four more horses refused to move an inch further, so we had to camp. People coming back on the trail told us that the cattle men were only a few miles further on, so I started out after supper to see if I could get any help from them. Walked seven or eight miles and found them at Moose Lake, about forty miles from Teslin. They had lost about sixty head of cattle, and were still looking for them. I sent the packer back the next day to bring my partner and his stuff along, but they were unable to pack any of his load further than the cow camp, so that he had to "cache" two horse loads of grub in the bushes, which I afterwards sent back for.

Leaving my partner in care of the cow men, I started off next day to see how things were going in Teslin. I thought I could reach Teslin that night, but at six o'clock in the evening was still some 15 miles short. The weather was getting cold and I had no grub or blankets, and "every prospect didn't please" (to reverse the old hymn) so I was glad when I came in sight of a camp. Three or four people were cooking supper, so I thought I had happened on a pretty good thing. I sat down, and asked what o'clock it was. (I knew only too well.) The people looked sour, and said, "Don't know, haven't a watch." I watched the bacon frizzling in the fry pan for a while, and asked again, "How far is it to Teslin Lake?" (I knew.) Answer, "Don't know, never been there." I thought they would not be missed in the place if they never got there either, and started off again; (it was getting dark).

After about four miles more, I came on another camp where there were two or three men and a huge fire. I asked how it was about a blanket or two. They said they were already entertaining a gentleman who had no blankets of his own. There was an old man across the creek who might help me out, but if he couldn't, I might come back, and they would do what they could. I crossed the creek and found an old man all alone, with two "burros" standing close to the camp. I found out later that they were the sole survivors of the fifty or sixty burros that had come over the Telegraph trail. I was getting humble now—the night was cold. I asked the old man if he could spare me a saddle blanket or two to roll up in. He said, "How?" I repeated. He put his hand to his ear and said, "I am a deef man." (A certain class on this continent always say deef instead of "deaf"). When I realized the situation I howled at him—the night was getting colder. He said, "Stranger you are welcome to half what I have got." Result, lots of bacon and blankets. That night one of the two burros died beside the old fellow's tent.

Next day I reached Teslin about noon in company with Johnny Harris and Jerry Gravelle, whom I found camped some eight miles front Teslin with their cattle. Harris and Knight had been building scows to take their beef down on and Jerry Gravelle, being short of the ready, was going to ship his beef along with theirs. Jack McIntosh, whom I had sent ahead had done good work, got together a crowd of men, and had them busily engaged in building scows for me. The man in charge of the sawmill at Teslin had

33

been making it rather warm for Mac as he had no money to pay for lumber used for the scows, the consequence being that Mac started out on foot to look for me; and of course missed me. He brought up however at the camp of the "burro" man (who told him that I had gone by), and returned to Teslin Lake where we met at last.

Probably the less I say of Teslin City the better. It was to have been a great town, but it wasn't. The government had taken possession of the townsite, and had almost given up the attempt to make people pay for a lot on which to erect a log cabin. The log cabin people numbered perhaps about one hundred, while along the shores of the lake were numbers of people camped in tents, who were building boats of all kinds, and vanishing down the lake as soon as they could get away. A steamer had been built at Teslin, which was to have plied between that place and Dawson. It went down the river, but could not get back, on account of low water. Had it been able to run, I could have got my beef down easily enough. I camped that night with one John McLeod, a Chilcoten neighbour, who had been packing some supplies from Glenora to Teslin Lake.

Next day (30th Sept^r) started back again to meet cattle, and tell them where to camp. The country was thickly wooded, (chiefly with useless scrubby timber), and camping grounds were scarce. Met my own private packtrain. Had to help it along to Teslin and returned 6 miles back on the trail with the horses to a place where I had told the cattle men to camp. Just arrived in time to find they had missed the feeding ground, and were all very cross.

Monday Oct. 3rd. Cattle lay over while I go to Teslin to arrange about a corral to butcher the beef in. By this time Harris and his men had built a corral and were going to butcher the next day.

Tried to work into Harris' corral, but he didn't want me. It was now a question [of] whether it would pay better to build another corral, or to wait till Harris was through. I tried, as I had done before,

LETTER TO HIS SISTERS

Teslin Lake,
4th Oct '98.

My dear Gals.

Just a line. The only chance to sell beef is to get it down to Dawson, so that we are building scows here and are going to kill the beef and try to get it down. It is freezing pretty hard and it is a question if I can get started before the lake freezes up. If it freezes up, I shall have to winter here and try to get the stuff down in the spring. I think I can get even on the beef sometime or other but it will take time.

I would like to write you a good yarn, but cannot manage it just now, as we have to be on the jump every minute. I have run rather short of funds but can just scare up enough to get down with. I am afraid I shall not be able to get out for some time—maybe June next year. If I can, you bet I will. This is the most pernicious country I was ever in.

Well be good to yourselves children and I'll come over and see you when I've sold the beef.

Got some letters from you at Telegraph Creek. No use to write again as I don't know where I will be.

> *With much love*
> *ever yours,*
> *Norman Lee.*

to get an opinion out of the cowpunchers, but they stared vacantly at me, and said nothing. Their brain power, which never had been great, had succumbed to much cowpunching on foot. I decided not to wait, but to begin butchering at a one horse butcher place, and then to move over to Harris' corral when he had finished.

I had sent two of my men back to get the stuff that had been left behind, three more were fixing up the place to butcher in, which left five men. Of these, two, who had hired to go all the way through with me, said that if it was all the same to me, they would like to return to Chilcoten, Jack Elliot, and Sheringham. They appeared to be almost silly from much cowpunching and night herding. Their eyes were bulging out of their heads and they did not seem to have an idea left but to get home as soon as possible. They evidently funked the trip down the river (Jack Elliot had been going to show me all along what a fine river man he was). I thought I could get along without them so let them go.

This left me with three men to hold the cattle. These gallant three had hired to me at Telegraph Creek, as they said they wanted to go to Dawson, and would not expect any wages till the beef was sold. They now approached me, saying that they would quit too, if I did not guarantee them a winter's grub when they got to Dawson. I could have got any quantity of men in Teslin who would have been glad of a passage to Dawson, but had no time to hunt them up, and did not like to put any strangers to herd the cattle, which might all have been lost, so I had to accede to their demands. I was now kept dancing about between the sawmill, where the scows were being built, and the butcher corral.

I found that I must procure still more grub, and was fortunate in being able to purchase some from John McLeod, at a twenty-five cent rate. Supplies bought at the stores had forty cents a pound tacked onto the Glenora price! A Doctor and his wife went into a store one day to enquire the price of sugar. The clerk replied, "sixty-five cents a pound." (The uninitiated may consider that a cent is equivalent to a halfpenny.) The lady turned to her spouse, and said, "I think, my dear, you will have to eat salt with your 'mush,' this winter." To which the storekeeper answered, "Salt will cost you sixty cents a pound."

When I say that the price of sugar at Victoria is about five cents a pound, and that of salt about half a cent, the gentle reader may be able to grasp the situation. My friend John was willing to sell me grub at the twenty five cent rate, but demurred at giving me time in which to pay for it. I have been trading with John for years, and have never seen the color of his money yet. However I induced him to take a draft at three months, which I arrived home just in time to meet. It made me rather sick to have to do so, as may be seen by a copy of the bill which I here produce, with prices of goods sold here attached.

John's Goods.				Chilcoten prices	
8 lbs Tea c 1°	$8.00			c 35	$2.80
1 doz Yeastpowder	9.00				3.00
130 lbs Beans c 32	48.00			08	12.00
50 " Rice c 32	16.00				5.50
350 " Flour c 31	108.50				21.00
100 " Sugar	36.00				10.00
50 " Potatoes evaporated	30.00			fresh.	50
40 " Salt c 3.	12.40				3.20
10 Onions evap.	6.00			fresh	20
1 can Yeastpowder	1.50				50
	$275.40				$58.70

A trifling difference of $216.70 and Chilcoten is supposed to be a very dear place to market in! Some few other things I had to purchase from strangers such as oakum, pitch, and ropes, for which I usually paid a dollar a pound.

How I ever got past Teslin, and the awful prices there, I hardly know to this minute, as I only arrived there with fifty dollars, which was equivalent to about fifty cents anywhere else. One might have a million dollars in the bank, but cheques were of no use in this country of strangers. However, I have lived through the ordeal, and shall keep away from Teslin for a while.

I had now to get rid of the horses, as we would not want them any more. One or two I sold for ten dollars apiece, but most of them went for seven dollars and a half a head, rigging included. The rigging alone cost me ten dollars or more for each animal. The purchaser gave me fifteen dollars down and said he would give me the rest when he saw me again. He never expected to see me, and I did not care if we never met so long as I could get safely to Dawson; but I met him later, and he has not paid me. The miserable sum he owed me was only twenty dollars (£4). He claimed to be a Colonel in the American Army, and to have thrown up a billet worth six thousand dollars a year in order to come to the country! I found out also that he belonged to the same party who were camped on the trail, and did not offer to feed me.

Up to this point I had been keeping a diary of events, but now let it drop, so have only a defective memory to refer to.

Harris had finished butchering his cattle, so I moved over to his corral, for the use of which I had to pay much money—an

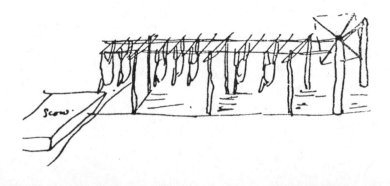

Scow.

abandoned corral that would be no use any more—but time was everything, so I had to pay. I hired an expert butcher to help us, who himself killed twenty head a day, while we managed twenty at our windlass. As soon as the cattle were killed, they were swung out onto skids which ran out over the river, so that the beef could be cut down and dropped into the scows. By the time the beef was all killed, the two scows were completed, and we soon had them loaded up.

Teslin lake is narrow at both ends. As the weather was getting cold, it was a great point to get the scows through the narrows before they froze over.

As it was, the scow men had to chop ice for half a mile, in order to get the scows down to the slaughter-house, some four miles from Teslin. As soon as we had butchered, the weather turned mild again. It rained every day, which did not improve the beef hanging in the open air. The beef was very poor, and at the best was not much more than bone. I had been obliged to buy two boats, one small one for going ahead and finding out channels and so forth. The other a species of small scow for carrying the beef over shallow places. The two scows measured each 16 feet by 40. The great thing was to get a fair wind down the lake, which was said to be about 100 miles long.

I think it was on the seventeenth of October that we started out and sailed gaily down the lake for two days with a fine fresh breeze behind us. The scow builders under McIntosh "ran" one scow; the other was managed by the cowpunchers under Will Copeland. I sailed along in the lighter. I had a stove going on each scow, so that food could be cooked without having to go on shore. On the third day the wind began to freshen, and we were tearing down the lake at a great pace. Waves were rolling high, and white caps were everywhere. About noon, I became aware that Mac was trying to get the scows to the shore. They were heavy unwieldy things, and hard to steer. I ran my boat up close to the scows, and noticed that they were shipping water. They were built like packing cases and were working back and forwards and sideways, and looked as if they would come to pieces. Mac was looking for some sheltered cove to run into, but shelter there was none, so to save the crew he ran the scows on shore, which happened to be rocky.

The waves were dashing over the scows and continued to dash, all that night, next day, and the night after. Some attempt was made to unload, but the men could not do much in the ice-cold water. In a few minutes one scow was broken in two, and the other had its side and end torn off. That night I slept not. The problem of what to do next was uppermost. It was too late to go back to Teslin and get new scows built, even if I had the funds to get them built with. It was not much use to save the beef even if it could be saved, as it was quite unmarketable where it was.

Next morning one of the men, a fussy Frenchman, came to me and said, "What are you going to do now?" I said, "I resign." "Then let us divide up the grub." I had quite a nice little supply of grub, and did not think that I was obliged to divide it amongst the crowd, but what did it matter, so I said, "Go for it." And they went for it. I never want to see such a scramble again.

Everyone had been asking everyone else what they were going to do. Some were for going down the river. Some were for going back. My two gigantic Missourians said, "Norman has brought us into the country, and he will have to see us out of it." There was hardly a man in the crowd that owned a dollar. I turned to the boys, and said, "I have five dollars in my pocket and cannot at present help you in any way. If you like to go down the river you can have the boats, but if you come back it is no use to look to me to help you out of the country." It was a case of "root hog or die." I knew that I alone could make my way, but that if the rest of the crowd came along, that they would stick to me like burrs, and would make it bad for all of us. The result was that every one except Will Copeland elected to go down the river to Dawson.

I told Will to see that we got a full share of the grub, which he did, though the others were inclined not to allow me any, as I had only sixty miles to go to get to Teslin, but I realized that food was money, so insisted on an equal share. I took a last look at the beef, and concluded that it was practically spoilt, as it had laid in the water for two nights and a day, and had then been dragged ashore through the sand with ropes, added to which it was nothing but skin and bone.

The rest of the men started to pull the scows to pieces, the idea being to make small boats, rafts, &c. and go on down the river. They had divided up into parties of twos and threes. Will and I took our grub, and one quarter of beef, and started to pull back to Teslin against a head wind. When we were some seven miles from Teslin (which took about four days to reach) we were stopped by ice, and had to pull our boat ashore. After deliberation, we left the boat, and loaded our goods onto a rough sled that we made with poles, and pulled this by slow degrees to within a mile of the town, when the thing refused to go any further. We pitched camp, and I left Will there, while I went on to town to see what to do next.

Before parting with the scows, I should have told you a story about the "Burro Man," whom you may remember. He wanted to go down to Dawson very badly and tried to get a passage down there with Harris on his scows, and with others who were going down in boats, but no one wanted him. At last he tackled me. We had some conversation in a high pitched key, and then I bawled at him, "I have all the men I require, I don't want you." With his hand to his ear, and a look of the most malignant cunning, he apparently caught on to the two last words and said, "Want me, all right I'll come." And come he did. He was between sixty and seventy years old, and I asked him what he would do if he were stuck down the river 300 miles from nowhere. "Oh," said he, "I'll manage." I thought, "You'll manage on my grub old party." So I asked him what supplies he had, to which he replied, "I've got plenty. I've got 95 lbs of flour to lend you." It turned out that he had 100 lbs of flour and was prepared to winter on 5 lbs, lending the other 95 to me. In the end of course he came, and whether he acted as a Jonah, I know not, but when the party broke up, no one wanted to take chances with the old man, and all tried to get him to go back to Teslin; but the old fellow was on his way to Dawson, and had not come there to go back, and at last was taken in tow by one of the party whom he found to be a member of a society to which he belonged. I presume the "Independent Order of Burro Men," but this was not explained to the uninitiated. So Uncle Harrison Hopkins vanished from my view.

Harris and Knight had pulled out from Teslin four days before us, so had apparently got away from the lake before the storm sprang up which caught us. Reaching Teslin in the evening, I fell in with a friendly saloon keeper. I had known this man slightly some 15 years ago and renewed acquaintance with him, when I first came to Teslin thinking that he might be of some use to me. He pressed me to stay with him that night. We talked over the disaster, and he found two or three men who believed that the beef was not all spoilt, and who thought they might yet be able to get it down to Dawson. I had not much faith in their schemes, as it was too late to build more scows then, and the question of freezing the meat and taking it down in the spring was a very doubtful one. However they had dogs, and sleighs, and might be able to take some of it over to Atlin (a place which was beginning to boom) though even that was a doubtful scheme on account of the distance.

Next day they started off with a dog team, and sleigh, on which they loaded their boat. I schemed hard not to go with them, as I was much spent and wanted a rest. So I stayed behind, borrowed a hand-sleigh and went down to the camp where I had left Bill. Together we hauled our stuff up to town to the saloon of my acquaintance. He made us welcome, and said that we could cook our grub on his stove, and taking us outside to a woodshed—"You can spread your blankets out there." A few minutes later his partner interviewed us. "Well boys, you can sleep on the floor in house," and trotting us out again to the pesky woodshed, "you can do your cooking out here." Taking a dose of each medicine, I concluded to cook in the house, and sleep there too—I hadn't lost any woodshed! And for about a week we had a much needed rest.

There was already some six or eight inches of snow on the ground, but the house of McInnis and Sabin was the warmest in the town, so we fared well. The saloons were hardly doing any business at all, and were chiefly frequented by pilgrims like ourselves who used the stove to cook their little messes on, and who slept on the floor at night. At one time in our hotel there were no less than five outfits cooking their food at the same time.

In about 6 days the men who had gone down to interview the beef returned, having had a very rough trip. They said that all the scow men had already got away, and had taken what beef they could with them. They found about thirty quarters that were fit for food, and the rest was spoilt by the water. They had been unable to get their boat down the narrow part of the lake on account of ice, so they used a part of one of my scows as a raft, loaded it with the thirty quarters of beef and started for home, using raw hides for sails. The wind and weather were very cold, and the raft was soon a mass of ice, but they managed to bring the beef within seven miles of Teslin. According to agreement I was to have one fourth of the beef, and was to be permitted to sell mine first if possible. So for the next three days Bill and I and the saloon man and one or two others hauled beef to town on handsleighs.

? Bill
? Me

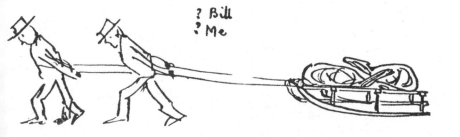

Having got the beef to town I busied myself trying to sell it, and in raising money by other means. Many people were willing to buy beef, but had no money. The town was full of beef. Whenever a work ox staggered into town from Glenora, with his last load on his back, a mass of sores and bruises from one end to the other, he was butchered and the meat was sold for ten cents a pound. That settled the price of beef. With difficulty I got rid of three quarters (the rest I presume are waiting to be sold yet). I got the dog-sleigh boys to pull my boat up to town on their sleigh, and sold it actually at a profit of 50 per cent. I sold one of the bags of flour that we saved for ten dollars (the store price was twenty) and as I wandered round, I found a man who took a fancy to my buckskin coat. This coat was just beginning to be the one thing needful to keep out the cold winds, but I had to raise the wind, instead of keeping it off. My friend offered me another coat and seven dollars in change. The deal was made. I hunted up another man who would buy coat number two. I worked him up to give me seven dollars and a half, and a bottle of whisky. I then trotted round till I found a gentleman willing to exchange a couple of dollars for the bottle. After selling one or two other trifles, I had amassed the princely sum of 85 dollars, and was ready to leave town.

Quite a number of people were preparing to leave Teslin with the idea of wintering at Telegraph Creek, as provisions were so much cheaper there, so we expected to have plenty of company. We waited a day or two longer for them, but I question if they have left Teslin yet. Bill and I tried to "rustle up" a handsleigh to haul our grub and blankets on, but could not get one, so Bill had to manufacture one, which he did very skillfully. Had we taken the trail to Skagway by way of Atlin, we would have got to the coast in fairly good time, but we did not know this road, while we knew the other (to Glenora) and also a great many of the people on it. Also we hoped that we would be able to get down the Stickeen river before it froze up, so we loaded up our sleigh and started out.

For five days we did about ten miles a day, the sleigh dragging heavily through the unbroken snow. This brought us to Moose Lake, where we found an English party who were building a cabin and going to winter there. One old fellow was an organist by profession and had never slept out of a bed before he started on this trip. His name was Lawes, and when I discovered that he hailed from Tollard Royal, he warmed towards me, invited us into the cabin and fed us. That night, snow came—thick heavy wet snow. I left a blanket or two with Mr. Lawes, also Bill and I parted with our overcoats, to lighten our loads.

In the morning we started again, but found the going very hard. The snow was three feet deep, and stuck to the sleigh till at last we could not lug it any further. So we had to abandon the sleigh, and throw away everything but our blankets and a little grub, and an axe. I threatened to throw away some more blankets, but Bill undertook to pack all the grub, and his blankets, if I would stay with mine. So we rolled our things up into the smallest possible space, and started off again, packing them on our backs.

Just before we started two fine Caribou crossed the trail about thirty yards in front of us. Of course we had no gun, and could not have used the meat if we had got it, and I think the Caribou knew it, as they were in no hurry to move on. This is the first time it has occurred to me to give you a picture of Robert-the-dog, who accompanied me in my wandering. Every other man that I met along the trail always said, "You had better give me that dog." It became rather monotonous after a while, especially as no one could give a reason why he should be specially selected as the recipient. It was fortunate for Robert that he was judged too small to pull sleigh, otherwise he might have fared worse.

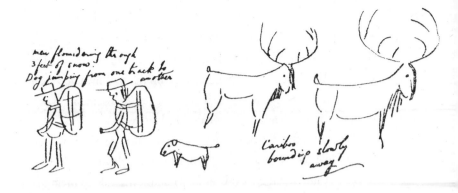

For two or three days or more, we wiggled on, packing our blankets, and camping at night in the snow till we came to the half way house, where was the Montreal outfit that I have mentioned already. They made us welcome, and helped us with tools &c, to make another sleigh, as the travelling had now become better. Starting again we got on fairly well though the thermometer in few days got down to 40 below zero, and a keen North wind blowing. We were fortunate enough at night to find houses to stop in and in a few days more arrived at Telegraph Creek, where Jim Cornell was still running his beef business. He had bought the restaurant as a means of selling his beef, and made us very much at home.

We stayed with him four or five days. He asked me to stay all winter, adding that it should not cost me anything. But it could not be, so we loaded up again and started for Glenora, where we expected to find some people who would accompany us down the Stickeen. Arriving there, we made ourselves much at home at the house of one Captain McPhatter, who had come over the Telegraph trail.

Captain McPhatter had the gift of the gab. I met him first on the trail near Hazleton, and he at once fired a volley at me—"What's your name where do you come from where are you going where were you raised" and without a pause "My name's McPhatter Captain McPhatter I hail from the East near Toronto I've been all over the world I've been in Australia &c, &c, &c, but withal the Captain treated us very kindly. I asked one of the men in his party whether he was a Captain or not—so many men on the trail invented their titles as they went along. He replied, "Oh yes, he's some kind of a Captain, right enough, or lieutenant Captain!"

We found that the Stickeen river was by this time frozen over, and navigation was impossible. People had fled down the river up to the last minute in all kinds of boats and rafts, among them my friend Sheringham, who was said to have upset and drowned. (Of course he didn't.)

Now, the question was whether the ice on the river was solid enough to carry us. We waited a day or two, and fell in with two people who wanted to go down. A Mr. Poore, (who incidentally told me that his brother married Dean Howson's daughter, possibly it was an invention) and a Col. W. W. Windward, who was one of the "main guys" of the "gipsy queen" outfit that had passed me by at Teslin, and had bought my horses. One night, Mr. Poore, who seemed to be a determined individual who would dare anything, came to us and said that he would start in the morning, and if we wanted to come we had better hurry up as he would go alone if we were not ready to start.

Now there are at least two ways to travel on the ice. One way is to have a sleigh for each man with a train of dogs pulling it, so that the men have nothing to do but jog along behind, while the fleetest man in the party runs ahead and thumps the ice with a pole to see if it is safe. At night a large tent is set up on the ice and a stove is kept burning inside, thereby enabling the owners to get dry and keep quite comfortable. This is the way for people who can afford to get dogs and other luxuries. The other way was the one we adopted. We could not afford a spare man to prod the ice, as it would take all our energies to pull the sleighs. Mr. Poore said he would have no objection to taking the lead all the way if we were afraid to try it. I never before had so strong a presentiment of impending disaster, but told Poore that we would go in the morning.

I went to a store to buy some snowshoes, which we should probably need, for myself and Bill, and was asked two dollars a pair for some that should be worth at least five or six. I thought that the store man must be losing on the transaction, so I treated him to a drink of whiskey. Then I found that he had bought the shoes from some pilgrims for a dollar a pair, and was clearing a hundred percent profit on the sale!

Next day Bill and I were up betimes, and waiting with our home made sleigh, loaded with blankets and grub, for the Colonel and Poore. These two were loath to start, as they had sat up all night playing cards and consuming stimulants. However we got away about ten o'clock. The ice being good, the gallant two got ahead of us as they had better sleighs and lighter loads. We went some ten miles and camped.

The days were now very short, and good firewood on the river banks was scarce, so that we had to look for a camping place about two o'clock in the afternoon of each day. Poore had told us that he had a good tent and a stove. The tent was barely large enough to hold Poore and the Colonel, who was a bulky personage, and the stove, which was all broken up, was altogether useless as it was impossible to get it inside the tent. A few days later it was abandoned.

Next day the ice got worse, and the danger increasing, Mr. Poore discreetly withdrew from his position as leader. The Colonel had not the least intention of risking himself, so that the job fell to my share, and I kept it almost all the way. It was by no means pleasant to plod along down the river through unbroken snow, hitched onto a sleigh, knowing that at any second one might tread on rotten ice, and disappear. And should one have gone through, that was the end.

The swift current, and the ice cold water would soon finish one off. As it was we each got in as far as our middles several times, but fortunately where the water ran slowly or was shallow.

We had been out about two days when snow began to fall—heavy wet snow that made travel impossible, so we had to lay by for four days. The last day rain came, and at night there was frost enough to make the going good again. We started off in a hurry, and managed to put about forty-five miles between ourselves and Glenora.

At dusk one day, when we were fixing our camp, we heard a jingling of sleigh bells, and with a rush and a whoop, along came four dog sleighs, and four men. This was an outfit that had started out from Glenora a week later than we had, taking the mail down to Wrangel and hoping to bring the incoming mail back. My friend McPhatter was in the party, which was led by a long legged Presbyterian "preacher." This man was much liked at Glenora and increased his popularity by his athletic tendencies. He was a well built wiry man, and was one of the record beaters in that part of the country, besides being a good fellow. We asked the dog men to camp beside us, but they laughed at us, saying they were going to do another ten miles that night. They started off at a swinging gait, and went one hundred yards, stopped dead, and came back, and camped with us; and their dogs sat on the edge of our tent all night and howled. The reason was that up to this point they had nothing to do but to follow our tracks as quickly as they could. Now that the tracks had come to an end, they had to proceed much more carefully.

Next morning we pulled out before the dog men, and reached a cabin, where were two men, in charge of a pile of goods that had got this far up the river on its way to Glenora. Our grub was getting rather short by this time, so we were glad to be invited to a square meal. Only the roof of the cabin could be seen, the snow on the land being 8 feet deep. This was the last place where we could purchase any supplies, so we tried to lay in a store, but were unable to secure anything but some musty oatmeal. We supposed that the men were too lazy to get us what we wanted, as they were "just out" of whatever we asked for. We arranged to stop the night at their cabin when along came the preacher and his outfit, armed with letters from high authorities, so that, late as it was, we had to turn out of the small cabin into the snow, and make place for his reverence and party.

It was no trouble for the dog party to make a camp as they could put their tent anywhere on the river, where there was very little snow, and put up their stove right on the ice. When *we* made camp we were obliged to lug our sleighs up the steep river bank onto the land. We had then to dig down through the seven or eight feet of snow, using our snowshoes for shovels, till we got down to the solid ground, whereon to build a fire. The hole so made was not very large, in fact was usually just big enough to allow of a fire being started. When fire wood was plentiful the hole would become large enough to allow of our getting into it, but when wood was scarce, we were obliged to sit round the top of the hole, and try to keep warm with the fire some five or six feet below us. On this particular evening, we travelled till it was quite dark, and found nothing better than rotten cottonwood, with which we had much difficulty to cook our food. Keeping warm was out of the question as the night was pretty cold, and we went to bed abusing the preacher to the best of our powers for ousting us from the cabin.

For several days after this we got along pretty well, keeping up with the dog trains, and one day beating them by three or four miles. We were delayed a good deal by the Colonel. He was a person wide in the girth, who had never been so far from whiskey and good living before in his life, and to whom the roughness of the journey came hard. It was very funny, though at the same time most aggravating, to see the comical little man making his first attempts

to travel on snowshoes. I would give something to have been able to have taken a few snapshots of my friend or even to be able to make a few graphic sketches of his antics. Of course he delayed us considerably, and to add to the difficulty he became ill and thought he was going to die, so that we had to camp early several times. All that ailed him was indigestion however.

After several days of good going, snow came again. Wet snow that made going almost impossible and made the ice more dangerous, so we went into camp again close to the preacher. For fifteen days and nights rain came and heavy wet snow that soaked our clothes and blankets through and through. We stayed in camp four days during which time the Colonel never moved out of his blankets; with the result that when we did start again, he was so weak that he couldn't travel very far in a day, thereby delaying us more than ever.

I took the opportunity to call on the "preacher" where I had a good warm and dried my clothes. The preacher outfit spent most of their time singing hymns, one of which seemed to me to suit the occasion. It was a dull monotonous refrain about a "weary land, a weary land, a refuge in the time of storm."

At the end of four days we held a council of war, and determined that we must go, as grub was getting very scarce. The preacher had started out with plenty of provisions, but his dogs took lots of feeding. He asked us to divide our supply with him, which we were loath to do, as we thought men should come before dogs. But I had got a little bacon from him earlier, so could not well refuse.

Next day we all started again, but could not get ahead more than four or five miles a day. Every day it rained or snowed, so that we were soaking wet all the time. Had it turned suddenly cold, we stood a good chance of freezing solid, as firewood was scarce. However we kept poking along, keeping pretty close up to the dog teams, until one day when the Colonel insisted on camping early, as he felt sick. There was now 8 or 10 miles of water and slush on the top of the ice, through which we had to pull our sleighs. Our grub was getting very scarce. In fact we had got down to 2 small plates of this "mush" a day, which did not tend to make us cheerful. The Colonel and Poore had tried to boss Bill and me more or less all the way, but at this stage of the game we cut them off short, and explained our views pretty strongly at times. At last one evening we arrived at a cabin at the junction of the Iskoot [Iskut] with the Stickeen.

The cabin was deserted, but seemed to offer a chance to dry out, as there was a good fire place in it and plenty of firewood all ready cut up, so we concluded to stop there for the night. We could tell by the tracks and so forth that the preacher had camped here the night before. We had got down to our last meal, which we proceeded to prepare. The Colonel advised that on the next day we should throw away our sleighs and blankets. and travel for all we were worth. The Colonel and Poore had both come up the river, in the spring, and should have known where we were, which turned out to be only about five miles from the Custom House at the Boundary between B.C. and Alaska, where some members of the Mounted Police were stationed.

While our food was cooking, and we were wrangling with the Colonel and Poore, suddenly we heard the report of a rifle. Looking

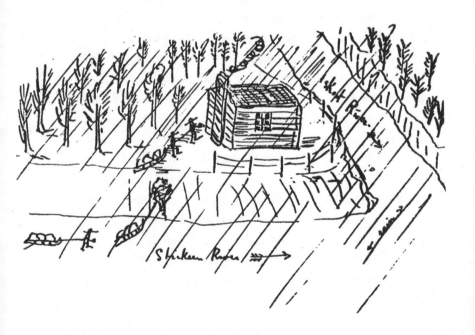

out onto the river we were able to make out in the distance a dog sleigh coming hastily up the river in our direction. We could not imagine who the newcomers could be, till a strapping youth in the mounted police getup trotted up to the cabin, and said that he constituted a rescue party. The preacher outfit had gone ahead as fast as possible and had reached the boundary at noon that day. They told the police that we were probably some fifty miles up the river, and would most likely be out of grub, so that within half an hour of their arrival, a sleigh was loaded with a month's supply of provisions, and despatched with two constables to meet us.

All was now joy and gladness. I treated Robert the dog to a whole dried salmon, which the poor dear wanted badly. (We had looked at Robert several times from a culinary point of view already, but he would have made thin soup.) Provisions were unpacked, the fire blazed; we accounted without delay for three cans of Sam Armour's excellent beef, and other dainties while Poore and I sat side by side, and cracked jokes, as though I had not threatened to chop him in two with the axe only ten minutes before. All this time of course it was raining day and night as hard as it could.

Next day we started off leisurely, and arrived through much water, at the station of the mounted police just in time for supper. We found here a Corporal Boldridge, and two constables (which I found to be the other name for "privates"), and in another building a U.S. Customs officer and his assistant. While the river was open they had a good deal to do, as all travellers had to call, pay duty and so forth, but just now, they had nothing to do but keep warm and were getting rather sick of the place. Here we were treated royally, and made up our minds to stay till the rain stopped. We were somewhat tickled also at being able to get something out of the government at last after all the years of tax paying. The mail outfit, who were not so fagged as we were, had kept going through the slush, so that there was plenty room for us all. The Corporal thought that eating was a bore, but we showed him that it was the one thing worth living for at that time.

And here I may make a statement respecting the appetite that I developed in the Northern country, and others have told they were affected in the same way. (Imaginary picture—inside of police barracks, blankets and clothes hanging up to dry. Warm stove. All hands tucking in grub.) From the time that I first "struck" Telegraph Creek till I got down to Wrangel, I was the victim of an appetite. Couldn't eat enough. Whenever food was plentiful, I might eat till I burst, and would still crave for food. An hour after a meal, I was starving again. And when I finally reached Wrangel after starving more or less for a month, I weighed twenty pounds more than I ever did before, and almost all the time I became so extremely inert and weary (what quack doctors call "the tired feeling") that it was quite an effort to drag myself about. Other people have told me that the climate affected them in the same way.

You can imagine our slow pace down the river when I say that the distance from Glenora to the Boundary is about 100 miles while we had left Glenora on the 2nd of December and spent Xmas day at the latter place. The police cook exerted himself and fed us on "plum duff," and other delicacies, among them beans swimming in syrup.

When we had stayed four days the rain stopped and a little frost made fine glare ice on the river. It was necessary to get more grub. Bill and I had already supplied more than our share, and had hauled it on our sleighs as well, but Poore said that he had no funds at present, and the Colonel would as soon starve as spend a ten cent piece, though he claimed to have thrown up a job bossing a big store in Chicago worth $6,000 a year to come out looking for gold. So seeing that there would be no grub, unless I got it, I applied to the Corporal.

He gave us food enough for a week, and gave me to understand that the Government did not accept money for such trifles.

We loaded up our sleighs and pulled out again. The ice was good and we did about fifteen miles. At night, of course, we camped where firewood was scarce, and next morning there was some coolness between us and the Colonel, because he had wanted to monopolize the fire, and we suggested there were others.

There was a keen wind blowing down the river, so Bill and I did not wait for the others who were dawdling but struck out at a run. Sometimes we put a canvas up on the sleigh for a sail and made great time, but by doing so we made a fatal mistake. We should have turned off the main river onto a "slue" [slough] which would have led us to Cottonwood Island, where several steamboats were wintering, and where a Chilcoten acquaintance of mine (Bill Jones) was residing with his lady. In the early spring when the rush began *up* the river, steamboats landed the pilgrims on Cottonwood Island.

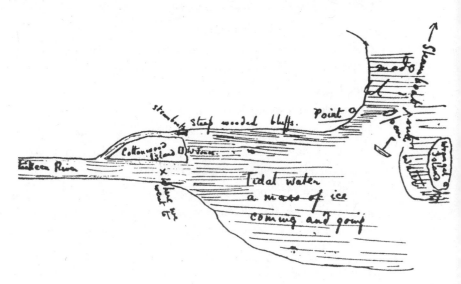

Most of them camped here more or less, till the condition of the river permitted them to start, consequently the Island was covered with all kinds of little houses, a big warehouse or two, and various sawmills, and boilers for engines that had been too heavy to haul up the river.

In our hurry down the river we forgot to watch for the preacher's tracks, which were still to be found now and then, missed the turn off down the slue and kept going till we came to an open expanse, covered with great floes of ice. As we did not know which way to go next, we thought to wait for the Colonel and Poore, and found it cold work. We tried to light a fire, but had to give up the idea, as all the wood we could find was water logged, and our fingers at last became too cold to strike a match. After waiting a couple of hours and seeing nothing of the other people, we thought something must be wrong, and retracing our steps on the other side of the river, against a biting cold wind, found the tracks of the others going down the slue. Started off again, but were stopped by finding that the tide was coming in, and was breaking up the ice.

While we were thinking what to do next, a dog sleigh overtook us. The Corporal from the Boundary, one of his constables, and one of the United States Customs men, had started a day after us with the intention of spending New Year's day in Wrangel. As they could not go any further that night, they pitched camp, and we stayed with them. Next morning, a couple of miles along the slue took us to Cottonwood Island, where we found Bill Jones, who gave us a good breakfast, and Mr. Poore, but no Colonel. These two had beaten us down the river after all, and had just arrived near the Island in time to see the steamboats, which would have been frozen in if they had stayed another day, pulling out for Wrangel, which was some eight miles off across salt water. The Colonel, on seeing the steamboats leaving, dropped his sleigh with all his possessions, and ran, singing out to Poore to look after the stuff, which he was just green enough to do, and just managed to catch a boat, which took him to Wrangel and whiskey that night.

Bill Jones made us welcome, and offered to lend us his boat to go to Wrangel in, but when put to the vote, it was thought to be too big a risk to start as the whole Channel seemed to be blocked with ice so we stayed chez Jones that night. Next day, Jones came to me and said, "If those fellows want my boat they will have to pay for it, before it leaves." The reason of this was that the channel was blocked worse than ever. (It was fortunate that Bill and I had not gone further when we missed the way the day before, as we had reached "tide flats" which would have been flooded in another hour.) The mounted police thought it impossible to get to Wrangel, so mournfully turned back to the Boundary, fighting their way against a cruel cold wind. Bill and I were determined not to go back if possible, so stayed with Jones till he found his grub getting short.

Fearing famine himself, he tried to ship us off in a "coffin ship," which in all probability would have finished us off, but we knew too much for that. Next day he told us that if we followed along the shore for five or six miles, the people in Wrangel would see, and come and fetch us. This plan we adopted. The shore was almost straight up and down and heavily timbered, so that we had to drop our sleighs, and pack on our backs. After the first day of this work, we held a council of war. We were making such slow progress that our small stock of grub would be gone by the time we reached the point, and if the Wrangel people did not see us, we should be apt to be pretty hungry. So we decided to turn back and live at Jones' expense; and it was well we did. We found out later that the town of Wrangel was round a corner where no one could have seen us. Of course Jones knew this—but anything to keep us from eating his small supplies.

59

When we got back to Cottonwood, he did not seem to be glad to see us, met us outside his house, and did not even ask us in to warm up. We took the hint, and hunted round till we found a little hut no more than six feet square and about five feet high. We got the preacher's stove which he had left on the Island, stuck it up, and proceeded to wait till time or circumstances should enable us to get to Wrangel. And here we sat huddled up in this little hut till our grub began to give out again. The hut was small enough, but we could get up a great heat in it, which was everything, as it was bitterly cold outside.

I went over one day to interview Jones about grub, but he would not sell me any as he was afraid of being short himself. I found out however that at the other end of the big warehouse where Jones was living, three or four other people were putting in the winter. These men were over in Wrangel celebrating the New Year, which festive season we had already enjoyed in Jones' house. When I found that they had plenty of food in their house, I marched boldly in and helped myself, so that we were once more in clover.

We were hoping every day that the Colonel would send a boat from Wrangel to take us from the Island, but he left us to our fate, and managed to get a steamer to take himself away to Chicago before we got a chance to talk to him. He did not even leave any message about the few dollars that he owed me for pack horses, nor did he even enquire my address. I took the pains however to find out his, and will write to him later!

In a few days more we were joined by four more pilgrims who had come down the river, and that night the people from Wrangel came back. They had been obliged to leave their boat some four or five miles along the shore on account of the ice, and had walked the rest of the way. We arranged with them to get the use of the boat and started off next day in high glee. We had to camp in the snow

one more night in order to accommodate the tide, and next morning rowed across to Wrangel where troubles may be said to have ended.

We found here the preacher and his mail outfit. They had had a rough trip from the boundary to Cottonwood Island through rain, and a foot of water. When they reached the slue which Bill and I missed, the tide was coming in, and the ice was broken up. Not wishing to camp another night, they boarded a large ice floe, dogs and all, and floated down to Jones' house.

The evening of the day on which we reached Wrangel, a steamboat left for Victoria. Bill wanted to go there, so I shipped him off, but waited myself, as I heard that a boat would leave for Vancouver direct next day, which was a consideration, as funds were getting short again; and as my clothes were in rags, I did not care to look up any of my aristocratic friends at Victoria. I had to stay in Wrangel 8 days before any boat of any kind came near the rotten place.

Pace seems to be slow in that part of the country; we had hung up on the river four and four, and four days, at Cottonwood Island only *ten*, and here eight (in all thirty days)—it seemed as if we never would get away; and all this time, I was in the biggest kind of a hurry to get home. The man in charge of my place might be playing ducks and drakes with the remnant of my estate, and running bills up into countless thousands. Though food was cheap in Wrangel, my funds became low again, as I had to stand the grub for two other men. One of them was on his way home to Edmonton (in the North West), and was short two dollars of the fare down the coast so that I had to see him to Vancouver, where he expected to find friends.

On the eighth day a steamer hove in sight. I boarded her without caring where she was bound for so long as it was somewhere South. Her destination was Seattle. How I was to get from there to Vancouver without funds I did not know or care. Not wishing to part with Bobber, the dog, and objecting strongly to buy[ing] a ticket for him, I was wicked enough to smuggle him on board. Robert seemed to realize the situation and sneaked on board, as if he had nothing whatever to do with me—but it was all to no purpose. I could find no place to hide him in, and in desperation had to confess to the purser, who made me buy a ticket with the alternative of turning Robert off the boat at the first stopping place, The fare luckily on the boat was cheap, and the grub was cheap—and nasty, but we survived. The boat fortunately had to call at Nanaimo to get coal, so that I left her one morning at four o'clock and after a walk of two or three miles was just in time to catch a steamboat which landed me in Vancouver, where we were pounced upon by many newspaper men. The papers next day had this statement, "Mr. Lee was among the passengers from the North. He declined to speak for publication."

I found myself in Vancouver with a roll of blankets, a dog and one dollar—the latter I took the first opportunity of exchanging for some refreshment, and made a fresh start with a clean sheet. Now came the advantage of having traded in Vancouver for years past. I went to see one of my merchant friends, who at once asked me "how I was fixed." I told him that I was stoney, so he hastened and got his cheque book and asked me how much I would like. He had just come out from Dawson himself, and told me that a big cattle outfit had been frozen-in about 200 miles up the river from Dawson. Thinking that he had got hold of the wrong end of my disaster, I confessed to him, but have since found out that Harris and his two scow loads of beef were caught in the ice, and the chances were very slight that he would get anything for his meat. This in a measure consoled me, as it would have been impossible for me to have reached Dawson, even if the scows had not gone to pieces in the storm.

After looking up one or two more merchants, and trying to find out how much I owed them without asking the question, I took the cars for Ashcroft, from which place, as the weather was cool, I started to walk up to Chilcoten, but getting weary called on my friend Doc English, who kindly loaned me a broken down crock, which conveyed me by slow degrees to the place of which the former proprietor said with tears in his eyes, "They called it a Chicken Ranch, but it was my home."

ABOUT THE AUTHOR

Well-known pioneer Norman Lee was born in England in 1862 and arrived in British Columbia in 1882, lured by tales of the Cariboo gold rush. After working at a variety of jobs in the Kamloops region, he settled in 1894 in Hanceville on the Chilcotin Plateau and got into cattle-ranching.

After his famous Klondike cattle drive of 1898, Lee returned to Hanceville, where he became a successful cattle rancher. He married his second cousin, Agnes, in England in 1902 and brought her back with him to the Chilcotin in 1903.

Norman Lee died in 1939. His descendents still live in the Cariboo, where the name Lee is almost legendary.